Boy Eats World!

To Leslie —
Eat the World!

Boy Eats

David
Lawrence
World!

A Private Chef Cooks Simple Gourmet

Lake Isle Press
New York

Published by:
Lake Isle Press, Inc.
16 West 32nd Street, Suite 10-B
New York, NY 10001
(212) 273-0796
E-mail: lakeisle@earthlink.net

Distributed to the trade by:
National Book Network, Inc.
4501 Forbes Boulevard, Suite 200
Lanham, MD 20706
1(800) 462-6420
www.nbnbooks.com

Library of Congress Control Number: 2006923880

ISBN: 978-1-891105-25-8
ISBN: 1-891105-25-6

Photography copyright © 2006 Tina Rupp

Book and cover design: Liz Trovato
Editors: Pimpila Thanaporn and Katherine Trimble

This book is available at special sales discounts for bulk purchases as premiums or special editions.
For more information, contact the publisher at
212-273-0796 or by e-mail, lakeisle@earthlink.net

First edition

Manufactured in the United States of America

10 9 8 7 6 5 4 3 2 1

"Approach cooking
and love with reckless
abandon."

—*The Dalai Lama*

"Food is the sustenance
of life that nourishes the
body, restores the spirit,
and soothes the soul."

—*Unknown*

Dedication

For the two women who taught me how
to cook:

Mom—It all started with you and your sense
of adventure in the kitchen. Thank you for
instilling that fearlessness in me and for
teaching me the magic of cooking. You
called it food, I call it love.

Aunt Harriett—You are the coolest aunt any
nephew could ever have. Thank you for the
best macaroni salad in the world and all of
your love.

I love you both.

Acknowledgments

Getting this book published started with a cold call to Lake Isle Press. I had just finished writing the first draft of my manuscript, and had read about this small New York publishing house, which was the first to take a chance on a then unknown Rachael Ray. The article went on to say that Rachael was an ambitious girl with not much more than a bunch of handwritten recipes and a dream, who'd gone on to tremendous and unprecedented success in the cookbook world. Inspired by her story, I took a deep breath and decided to make the call.

Figuring I had nothing to lose, I boldly launched into my pitch. As it turned out, the woman to whom I had been rambling on about was Hiroko Kiiffner. The publisher! I like to think she was charmed by my chutzpah. By the end of our chat she asked me to send her my manuscript. I did, immediately. But getting to the next step wasn't as easy. It turns out I wasn't quite ready to be published. I had a lot of work to do, but the advice Hiroko gave me was invaluable. It took about a year, but with persistence, patience, and a willingness to apply the lessons she taught me, I finally got the call. Lake Isle Press was going to publish *Boy Eats World!* It was truly one of the most exciting days of my life.

Thank you Hiroko for answering the phone that day and not hanging up! Thank you for believing in my talent, for your patience, for your willingness to take a chance on me and my dream, for helping me grow, for sharing your wisdom with such grace, and for making my dream of publishing a cookbook come true. Thank you also to the key members of your team at Lake Isle Press, Kate Trimble and Pimpila Thanaporn, for their ideas and enthusiasm.

Many more people have helped take this book from dream to reality:

Allen Schmitt, thank you for putting up with me when it got crazy, for believing in me always, and for never complaining no matter how messy the kitchen got. The website rocks! You have enriched my life in immeasurable ways. Thank you for standing next to me through not only this book, but in life. I love you. John Berndt, for believing in my crazy notion to write a cookbook from the start. Even when I didn't always believe in it myself. Thank you for your brutal honesty about all things, from food to life. I am a better person for knowing you. You are the very definition of a best friend. Adrienne, my sister, my friend. You're truly one of the coolest people I know. I'm going to turn you into a cook yet! Bradley Bernstein, my manager, thank you for taking a chance on me and learning a whole new area of the business, for your tireless efforts on my behalf, for talking me "out of the tree" a lot! For always looking out for and guiding me. You're more than a manager, you're a real friend. Lisa Queen, my literary agent, thank you. Duane Poole and Frank Bonaventure, thank you for your love and support and for kindly letting a camera crew take over your beautiful kitchen. Twice! Joel Dean, thank you for your encouragement and friendship. In many ways my success can be traced to you. Now if only I can get you to represent cooking talent! Tina Rupp, for your beautiful photographs. You're an artist with an uncompromising eye. Korina Jochim, thank you for the incredible opportunity to write for your magazine. You give me so much freedom to express myself. Thank you for your faith in my writing ability and for always taking such care with my words. You're a dream editor! Monique Hart, thank you for your friendship, patience, and advice. You've been on this journey with me from the beginning and always believed it was possible. You've taught me so much about the business of the business. I'm grateful to have a friend and mentor like you. Marc Summers, one of the nicest guys in the business. I'm grateful for your wisdom. Natalie Haughton, for all of the food chat and for that great article in the Los Angeles Daily News. I'm glad to know you. Michelle Sedlacek, you're a great makeup artist. Thank you for making me feel comfortable, for keeping the energy up, and always being so much fun. Thank you to Taji Marie, and all of the wonderful staff at Sur La Table in Los Angeles for your enthusiasm and support of this project. You're all such a pleasure to work with! Rene Solem, at Gelson's Market in Los Angeles, thank you for giving me the opportunity to teach and develop my skills in such a supportive environment. J.T. Seaton, thank you for the great photos for the website. Your work is beautiful! Tom Trellis, and the staff at The Alcove Café in Los Angeles, thank you for letting us shoot in your beautiful café and for making us feel so at home. Sara Henry, I got to know you as an editor and now I consider you a friend. Thank you for your advice and friendship. Someday we'll actually meet in person! The Rubin family, Nathan, Michele, Natasha, Camille, and Adam, I owe so much to you guys. Thank you for all that you've done and continue to do in support of my career. You were the guinea pigs and taste testers for many of the recipes in this book. You have truly made me feel like a part of your family. I love you guys!

I'd also like to thank the people who've influenced my work, all of whom I've never had the pleasure of meeting, but hope to someday. Ina Garten, your beautiful food and easy style inspire me to no end. I treasure your books. Martha Stewart, you paved the way for all of us. You're a true inspiration in life, in business, and in the kitchen. Rachael Ray, the best 30 minutes on television! You've taught me so much.

Contents

Introduction *10*

Kick-Starters *23*

Souped Up *59*

The Main Attraction *73*

Sidekicks *121*

Childhood Favorites *141*

Just Desserts *159*

Mixology *187*

Index *201*

When Worlds Collide

I'm often asked what my food specialty is. To be honest, I don't really have one. I just love food! Period. Love to cook it, love to eat it. Of course, I have my favorites, but my culinary tastes are quite literally, all over the map. My personal approach to cooking borrows from different cultures, palates, and styles.

I grew up eating simple country food, based largely on the Southern-style cooking of my grandmother and her mother before her. There was always a coffee can of bacon grease in our refrigerator used for frying up everything from eggs and hash browns, to T-bone steaks. My mom was adventurous in the kitchen (that must be where I get it) and was always eager and willing to try new ideas and experiment with different flavors. She would (and still does) read cooking magazines and the newspaper food section in search of inspiration. She was also a big fan of cooking shows and Martha Stewart long before Martha was fashionable, unfashionable, and fashionable again.

I can recall instances when my mom's excitement at trying a new recipe or developing one of her own, would quickly turn to disappointment if it didn't turn out quite the way it was intended. A few of them we ate anyway. Quite happily, I might add. Whether her efforts were successful or not, watching her fearlessly tackle new recipes really influenced how I approach food today. It laid the groundwork for lots of kitchen adventures to come.

When I moved to Los Angeles ten years ago, I was introduced to a whole new world of tastes and culinary possibility. Like all major cities, Los Angeles is a melting pot of people and cultures, and it was only a matter of time before those influences found their way into my cooking. It was here that I first tasted Middle Eastern food, sushi, and fish tacos. Those experiences fueled my desire to cook for a living and share my passion for food with people.

As a private chef, I have to tailor menus and recipes to specific clients. It's a challenge that never gets old. Every client wants something a little bit different. Whether it's a simple dinner for the family on any given Tuesday, or an elegant dinner party for ten on Saturday night, complete with cocktails, hors d'oeuvres, and several courses. No matter the occasion, I always approach it with the same enthusiasm.

In the beginning of my career, when I was scrambling to establish myself in a competitive market, I would never admit that I had never heard of a dish a potential client was requesting, or that I had absolutely no idea how to prepare it. I was too afraid of losing the job! Instead, I nodded enthusiastically and sometimes stayed up all night testing variations of the recipe. It was definitely a sink or swim environment. Happily, I'm still afloat!

As I gained more confidence and experience, I started to mix things up in the kitchen, experimenting with flavors from different cultures or taking a familiar favorite and adding an unexpected twist. That includes many parties I've catered. I wanted the recipes in this book to reflect that same spirit of globetrotting. From decidedly American dishes as fried chicken and macaroni salad, to Asian-inspired dishes such as tom kha gai and Vietnamese spring rolls. Or, my take on French food made easy, such as chocolate soufflé or potato gratin.

Food is a universal language we all understand no matter where we come from or what our background. I have a tremendous passion for food. I want to share that passion with you. I hope the thoughts and recipes in this book will inspire you to try something new, to explore new flavors, and to get out there and Eat the World!

It's All About Having Fun

People who don't cook seem to think that people who do practice some sort of kitchen witchcraft. I've seen the look of sheer panic cross their faces at the mention of words like deglaze, reduction, seared, or crusted. True, these words may seem big and scary at first, but once you learn a few basics, they are no longer words to fear. As with anything in life, the more you cook, the more confident you become. If I have one goal, it's to inspire people to start cooking, to develop their "culinary confidence." The kitchen is a place I hope to demystify. The way I see it, it's a place to play, to create.

This book is intended to familiarize you with the basics. Most of the ingredients are easily found in a regular grocery store with the exception of a few specialty items. If you've never attempted cooking before, I would advise you to start small. Baby steps. Don't try to tackle dinner for ten the first time you set foot in the kitchen. Instead, be realistic. Try cooking for two instead. Choose dishes that appeal to you and use familiar ingredients and flavors. Once you begin to feel confident, try branching out. Having friends over for dinner doesn't mean you have to whip up some exotic, fancy meal worthy of the best five-star restaurant. Don't let your eyes glaze over at the mere thought of throwing a dinner party, saying, "Oh, I could never do THAT." I say, "Yes, you can."

Welcome to the Kitchen

One of my favorite culinary urban legends is the one about the young bride who dutifully sets about preparing a Sunday roast for her new husband and cuts off the ends of the meat before cooking it. The confused husband eats the roast and thinks it's delicious, but can't help inquiring about the strange practice. The wife shrugs and matter-of-factly replies, "That's how my mother always did it." Now curious about the reason, the young bride asks her mom whose reply is simple. "I never had a pan big enough for the roast, so I cut the ends off!"

This tale illustrates our willingness to go along with things without question. Especially when it comes to culinary matters. Otherwise perfectly logical people easily fall into the "because that's how my grandmother, aunt, mom, uncle, sister did it" trap. When I teach cooking classes, the questions most often have to do with personal taste. It's always, "Can I use chicken instead of beef in that recipe?" Or, "What if I don't like asparagus, can I use broccoli instead?" My answer is always a resounding and enthusiastic, "YES! Of course you can!" Trust your instincts and your taste buds.

The recipes here are intended as a jumping-off point to get you into the kitchen. They are based on my preferences, but feel free to add your own personal touches. For example, if you find you don't like a certain ingredient, such as cilantro, then by all means, leave it out. Maybe try replacing it with flat-leaf Italian parsley for a milder flavor. Allowing yourself to experiment, adding a pinch of this and a dash of that, will set you free. Not to mention, it's a lot more fun.

The only time I would insist that you follow a recipe to the letter is in baking. Baking is chemistry, whereas cooking is personal expression. Baking is a formula that must be followed precisely to achieve the best results. It's the one time in the kitchen you can't get away with "fudging it." (Pardon the pun.) They say you either cook or you bake. I happen to enjoy both. Admittedly, chemistry was never my best subject. Baking somehow redeems me, gives me a feeling of competence in a chaotic world, and when my soufflé rises, makes up for a lifetime of not paying attention in class.

A Few Words About Kitchen Equipment

I'm convinced that people shy away from cooking, in part, because they don't have decent kitchen equipment. It's no fun to do anything without the proper tools for the job. I'm not suggesting that you need a kitchen full of expensive, state-of-the-art equipment to make dinner. But you do need a few basics. As a private chef, I've had the opportunity to cook in many home kitchens, and I'm constantly amazed that people will spend major amounts of money remodeling their kitchens, thousands on a new stove, and months deliberating over the perfect wall color, yet they won't invest a couple of hundred dollars on decent kitchen knives. (I always travel with my own set.) Take my advice and sink a few dollars of your hard-earned fortune into a set of high-quality, full-tang kitchen knives. You don't need to buy the most expensive set on the market, but at the very least, purchase a good-quality butcher knife, a paring knife, and a good serrated bread knife. To maintain the quality of your knives, take them to a professional sharpener occasionally, or use a sharpening whetstone at home to keep them razor sharp. If you've ever tried to saw through a tomato or force a dull, flimsy blade through a

piece of citrus, then you know how dangerous a dull blade can be. A good set of knives will last a lifetime if properly cared for, and they will become indispensable.

The same is true for cookware. Again, you don't need to buy the most expensive set on the market, but there is nothing worse than cooking with flimsy pots and pans. If you've ever tried it and ended up with less-than-desirable results (burned or scorched food), you see the need to outfit your kitchen with a few good-quality items. To cover the basics, you'll need a frying pan, a flat-bottom sauté pan, a 2-gallon stockpot, and two saucepans (1 to 1 1/2 quarts and 3 to 4 quarts). A nonstick skillet is also a good idea; I couldn't live without mine for making omelettes and frittatas. An enameled cast-iron Dutch oven (an ovenproof pot with two handles and a tight-fitting lid) is a bit of an investment and can be added as needed, but it's practically indestructible and will last a lifetime. Look for cookware that is heavy for its size and has a good thick bottom; heat will be distributed more evenly, ensuring better cooking results.

Also, cookware with ovenproof handles is a good idea, so you can take your cooking from stovetop to oven with ease. Cooking is so much easier and enjoyable when you start with the right equipment. I promise you, it is well worth the investment. Happy cooking!

A Few Helpful Kitchen Tips

Fresh vs. Dried Herbs—I use fresh herbs whenever possible in my cooking. It makes such a big difference in the flavor of a dish. Fresh herbs are readily available in most major grocery stores, and they are relatively inexpensive. There are two simple rules of thumb when using fresh herbs as opposed to dried. First, if a recipe calls for dried herbs and you opt to use fresh, use twice the amount, as dried herbs are more concentrated in flavor. Second, unlike most dried herbs, which are added at the beginning of a recipe (to allow the flavors to develop), you add fresh herbs at the end so they keep their color and vibrancy. When using dried herbs, crush them up in the palm of your hand before adding them to the dish; this helps release their flavors.

One more thing: All herbs and spices have a shelf life, and I hate to break it to you, but it's relatively short. Over time, they actually lose their potency and flavor. Herbs and spices need to be rotated every six to eight months, which is why I recommend buying the smallest jar possible. Avoid the temptation to buy these things in bulk.

Freshly Cracked Black Pepper—Get rid of that red and white can you have sitting in your spice cupboard! It's nothing more than sneezing powder. There is absolutely no substitute for freshly cracked black pepper. This is the reason any decent restaurant has an eager waiter standing over you with a pepper mill the size of a baseball bat. True, it adds a bit of showmanship to the whole affair, but more importantly, it just tastes better!

Kosher Salt—This stuff is a revelation! For my everyday cooking there is nothing else. The flavor of kosher salt is much softer than iodized table salt. Also, it's indispensable for creating a crusty coating on seared meats and for finishing off vegetables with a bit of salty crunch.

Canned Stocks—I am not a fan of hours and hours of intense labor, in the kitchen or anywhere else. For this reason, I am a big fan of canned chicken, beef, and vegetable stocks. There are several good brands out there, and they really have come a long way. While you could make your own stock by boiling chicken carcasses and root vegetables all day long, using a good commercial stock will definitely save you lots of time. About five hours to be exact.

Frozen Peas—I know we've all been told that fresh vegetables are the only way to go, and that is true—with one exception: peas. This is the one vegetable that is surprisingly better when purchased frozen. That's because peas are picked at their peak of freshness and flash-frozen so they can be enjoyed all year round. Peas are tricky to purchase fresh. Once they're picked, the clock is ticking; their high sugar content turns to starch very quickly (45 percent within three hours, if not refrigerated) and the result is mealy and unappetizing. Even in season, there is no telling how long they've been sitting on a grocer's shelf. Why risk it? I always use frozen peas.

Canned Seasoned Bread Crumbs—It's definitely no big deal to make your own breadcrumbs. Just blitz up some stale bread in a food processor. But when it comes to seasoned breadcrumbs, well, that's an altogether different matter. It's difficult at best to get the balance of seasonings right (believe me, I've tried), so why fight it when all the work has already been done for you?

Real Whipped Cream—There are few things in life that I am a flagrant snob about—whipped cream is one of them. I do not understand why anybody would buy plastic "whipped cream" in a can or a frozen tub. It bears absolutely no resemblance to the real thing, and there is nothing appetizing about it. It takes no time at all to whip up a bowl of fresh cream, with a little sugar and a splash of vanilla. It actually takes longer to thaw the frozen stuff. Your palate and your guests will thank you.

A great trick for keeping fresh whipped cream from breaking down and getting watery is to stabilize it with a marshmallow. Whip the cream as usual until soft peaks form. Whip in one large marshmallow that has been softened for about 10 seconds in the microwave. The result is whipped cream that will last longer than you do.

Fresh Lemon and Lime Juice—There is no substitute for freshly squeezed lemon or lime juice. Please steer clear of so-called citrus juice that comes in a plastic squeeze bottle. It only takes a second to cut open and squeeze a fresh lemon, and the flavor is so much brighter. Anytime you can use fresh ingredients in your cooking it will make a big difference in the final outcome.

Unsalted (Sweet) Butter—You've got two choices when it comes to butter: salted and unsalted. Salt is added as a preservative to extend the shelf life of butter (about five months, as opposed to three for the unsalted variety) and to mask any impurities or odor. The salt interferes with the natural sweetness of the butter and makes it difficult to know how much salt you need to add to a recipe, especially since the amount of salt can vary depending upon the brand. It may seem obvious, but you can always add more salt; you cannot take it away. For this reason, I always use unsalted butter in my cooking.

Pasteurized Egg Product—Some of the recipes in this book call for the use of raw eggs. There is some concern about salmonella and raw eggs. I always advise people to use only the freshest eggs from a source they feel confident about. If you are pregnant, nursing, or in poor health, you may want to consider some alternatives. In some larger markets they sell eggs that have been pasteurized in their shells for just such recipes. If you can't find them in your area (I live in L.A. and I've had to search for them), you can use a pasteurized egg product. They are 100 percent real eggs and are usually found in the refrigerated dairy case. Use of this product will not affect the taste or texture of your finished recipe.

Fresh Egg Test—If you ever find yourself questioning the freshness of an egg, there is a simple test you can do to put your mind at ease: Place the egg in a bowl of water deep enough to cover the egg by about an inch. If the egg lies flat horizontally it is impeccably fresh. If it rises up slightly, it is still fresh but probably about a week old. If it stands up vertically (large end up) it's probably seen better days (2 to 3 weeks old). If it floats completely, get rid of it! If you're curious about why the egg floats, it's because the egg has an air cell inside of it that gets bigger with age. The bigger the cell, the more buoyant the egg.

Folding Egg Whites—To take the fear out of folding egg whites into a batter, you can use an electric mixer on low speed to gently incorporate them without risking deflation.

Electric Mixers—In recipes requiring the use of an electric mixer, you can use either the free-standing or handheld variety.

Instant-Read Meat Thermometer—I simply can't imagine life without this handy kitchen tool. It's the easiest, most efficient way to ensure that your meat is cooked to the proper internal temperature. There are ways of testing doneness by feel of the meat, but unless you spend your days hovering over a restaurant grill and have become incredibly adept at testing for doneness this way, it's best to stick to an instant-read thermometer.

Carryover Cooking—All meat and poultry should be allowed to rest, loosely tented under some foil, for several minutes after it is cooked to allow the juices to redistribute and the meat to relax. The meat will continue to cook after it has been removed from the oven or the grill, and the internal temperature will go up any-where from 5° to 10°F, depending on the size and density of the meat. This is known as carry-over cooking; keeping it in mind will help ensure that you don't end up with dry, overcooked meat.

Internal Temperatures for Red Meat—There are many opinions on the best way to cook steak. As a true steak lover, I prefer mine medium-rare. Searing a steak beyond medium cooks out the natural juices, fat, and in my opinion, taste. You should, of course, cook your steak exactly as you like it. For rare meat, cook to an internal temperature of 120° to 130°F; medium-rare, 130° to 140°F; medium, 140° to 150°F; and well-done, 160°F.

Sifting Dry Ingredients—For some reason I loathe the chore of sifting together dry ingredients for baked goods. So I was thrilled to discover that you can get the same result by simply whisking the dry ingredients together with an ordinary wire whisk.

Parchment Paper—Another invention I simply cannot be without. Parchment paper takes away the need to grease your sheet pans, makes

cleanup a breeze, and ensures that your food won't stick.

Heat-Resistant Rubber Spatulas—Made of silicone instead of the traditional rubber, these little things can withstand heat up to 400°F or more (depending on the brand). An absolute must for making perfect scrambled eggs! You can stick with the old-fashioned rubber kind if you must, but when the end of it begins wearing down after lots of use in a hot pan, where do you think that rubber ends up?

Two Low-Fat Baking Substitutes—On those occasions when I feel I've had a little too much indulgence and I need to lighten things up a bit, I have a couple of low-fat baking substitutes that I find useful. First, two egg whites make a fat-free alternative to one whole egg. Second, an equal measure of applesauce can be used to replace the oil in any baking recipe. Trust me, no one—not even you—will detect any difference in the outcome of the finished baked goods.

Olive Oils—If I were to go on about the differences in olive oils from virgin to extra-virgin to fine-virgin, not only would my head start spinning, I would have to write another book! Just keep the following in mind: Extra-virgin olive oil comes from the first pressing of olives and contains a very low level of acidity. It has a low smoking point (it burns fast) and is best used for light sautéing, as a condiment for dipping breads, or in dressings and sauces so its natural fruitiness can be appreciated. Regular olive oil has a much higher smoking point and can be used in place of other fats like butter or corn oil for cooking and frying. To keep things simple, I always buy and use extra-virgin olive oil in all my recipes, unless otherwise stated.

A Few More Helpful Kitchen Tips

- Never refrigerate tomatoes, potatoes, onions, or garlic. Store tomatoes at room temperature for better flavor; potatoes, onions, and garlic last longer in a cool, dark place.

- If a recipe calls for half an onion, save the root half. It lasts longer.

- Keep berries refrigerated uncovered until just before serving, then rinse well and drain in a colander or sieve.

- You will get almost twice the amount of juice from citrus fruit if you microwave it for ten seconds before squeezing.

- To clean mushrooms, simply wipe them with a damp cloth, or dust them off with a pastry brush. Never run mushrooms under water. They're like little sponges and will soak up all that liquid and become waterlogged.

- Leeks grow in loose, sandy soil and must be cleaned properly before using. I generally cut them in half lengthwise, slice them thin, and swish them around a bowl full of cold water. All of the grit will drop to the bottom. Dry thoroughly on paper towels.

- To peel ginger, use the edge of a spoon and move it along the curves of the root as if you're carving it. You'll be surprised at how easily the skin comes off, preserving the delicate flesh within.

- To keep the water in a pot of noodles or rice from boiling over, add 1 tablespoon oil to the water.

- Always salt pasta water after it has come to a boil. The Italians say, "It should be as salty as the Mediterranean Sea," and it's the only chance you have to season the pasta itself. Salt raises the boiling temperature of water and if added to a pot of cold water it will just sink to the bottom and "scar" your pot.

- If you've over-salted soup or vegetables, add cut, raw potatoes and discard them once they have cooked and absorbed the salt.

- Fresh celery leaves dropped in a pot while cooking shrimp helps destroy the odor.

- Got something burnt onto the bottom of a pan and absolutely can't get it off? Add enough water to cover the bottom of the pan along with 1 cup white vinegar. Boil for ten minutes. The burnt food should wipe right out.

- Hard-boiled eggs will peel easily when cracked and placed in cold water immediately after boiling.

- A quick test to make sure baking powder or baking soda is still good: Place a teaspoonful into hot water. If it fizzes, it's still good.

- Spray measuring spoons with nonstick cooking spray before measuring something sticky, like honey or molasses. It will slide right out and give you an accurate measure.

- Chopped fruit and nuts will be more evenly dispersed in cake batter if tossed with a bit of flour before adding.

- One of my favorite tricks for getting cakes out of a pan without greasing and flouring is to line the bottom with a sheet of paper towel. To get a perfect fit, trace the cake pan on the paper towel and cut out. When you tip the cake out of the pan, the paper towel peels right off!

- Eggs will beat up fluffier if they are allowed to come to room temperature before beating.

- Cream, on the other hand, will whip faster and fluffier if the cream, bowl, and beaters are well chilled.

- To get rid of the garlic smell on your fingers, just hold your hands under running water while rubbing them on anything made of stainless steel. A spoon works well.

- After grating cheese, rub a hard crust of bread over the grater to clean it.

- In culinary school, would-be chefs are taught to flip food in a pan by first practicing with a slice of bread to help them get the flipping motion.

- There are two ways to open a bottle of bubbly: For drama and flair you can shoot the cork at the ceiling. (It's only funny until someone loses an eye. Then it's hilarious!) My preferred method is to slowly twist the bottle, not the cork, without making a sound.

- I heard, once upon a time (and I'm not sure if this is entirely accurate), that cooking wine was invented to keep chefs from imbibing while they were supposed to be cooking. It is incredibly salty and filled with additives that make it practically undrinkable. Keep in mind that the flavor of alcohol doesn't improve when you cook it down; it intensifies. So if you wouldn't drink it out of a glass with your dinner, why on earth would you reduce it down and concentrate that flavor in your dinner? If it tastes bad in the bottle, it'll taste bad in the dish.

- To toast nuts, place them in a dry sauté pan and push them around over medium heat until they begin to deepen in color and their nutty aroma begins to waft up under your nose. Once they begin to toast they go quickly, so whatever you do don't abandon them. They go from perfectly toasted to "toast" in a matter of seconds.

- One of the coolest trade secrets I learned in my catering days was the technique of "marking" a piece of meat on the grill and finishing it off later in the oven. This simply means placing the meat on a hot grill just long enough to get those beautiful criss-cross grill marks, leaving it completely raw in the center. If I'm hosting a party at home, I mark the meat several hours before the start of the event and finish cooking it through in a 400°F oven to desired done-ness. The benefit is two-fold: You don't have to sweat over a hot grill in the middle of your own party, and the meat comes out incredibly tender and juicy.

Kick
Starters

Collective wisdom tells us, "You never get another chance to make a first impression." When I plan a dinner party, one of the first things I do is figure out the best way to kick-start the meal. In this chapter you'll find recipes from the simple to the sophisticated, perfect for casual buffets or more formal, sit-down dinners.

Goat Cheese Torta Strata

makes 3 cups

I'm mad about goat cheese! For that reason this appetizer is one of my favorite things to make for casual get-togethers with my friends. It's very "California," and it's always a hit! The best part about this recipe is that except for roasting a head of garlic, there's no cooking involved.

1   head garlic

Extra-virgin olive oil, for drizzling

Kosher salt and freshly cracked black pepper, to taste

1/2   pound cream cheese, room temperature

1/2   pound goat cheese, room temperature

1/2   cup sun-dried tomato pesto

1/3   cup basil pesto

Preheat the oven to 400°F.

Slice the top off the head of garlic, drizzle with oil, and sprinkle with salt and pepper. Wrap in foil and roast in the oven until the garlic is soft and caramelized, about 1 hour.

Meanwhile, in the bowl of a freestanding mixer fitted with a paddle attachment or with a hand-held electric mixer, cream together the cheeses. Divide the cheese mixture evenly among three small bowls. Add the sun-dried tomato pesto to one bowl; add salt and pepper and mix to combine evenly. Add the basil pesto to the second bowl; add salt and pepper and mix to combine. Squeeze the roasted garlic cloves into the third bowl; add salt and pepper and mix to combine.

Line a 3-cup ramekin with dampened cheese-cloth*, draping excess over the rim. Spoon basil pesto mixture into the bottom of the mold and smooth with a rubber spatula. Top with the roasted garlic mixture, and finish with the sun-dried tomato pesto mixture. Fold the excess cheesecloth over the top of the strata. Refrigerate for at least 1 hour.

To serve, unfold the cheesecloth, invert the ramekin onto a platter, and peel away the cheesecloth. Serve with your favorite crackers, Melba toast, or crudités.

*Cheesecloth is easy to find at most grocery stores, kitchen-supply stores, or even some hardware stores. In a pinch, you could probably use a paper towel or plastic wrap, but cheese-cloth is best and adds a cool, artisan-like texture to the finished mold.

Sweet-and-Sour Cocktail Meatballs

makes about 25 meatballs

These are those retro-kitsch meat-balls from the days of yore, dating back at least to the days when Carter was in office. I remember fondly the chic holiday cocktail parties my mom would throw with plenty of these meatballs keeping warm in a Crock-Pot. Okay, maybe the Crock-Pot wasn't so chic, but it was the seventies! I always loved the notion that the "sweet" part of the sauce came from ordinary grape jelly. A very cool thing when you're 6 years old!

FOR THE MEATBALLS

- 1 pound ground sirloin
- 1/2 cup plain bread crumbs
- 1/3 cup chopped onion
- 1/4 cup milk or half-and-half
- 1 large egg, lightly beaten
- 2 tablespoons minced fresh flat-leaf parsley
- 1/2 teaspoon Worcestershire sauce

 Kosher salt and freshly cracked black pepper

FOR THE SAUCE

- 1 (12-ounce) bottle mild chili sauce
- 1 (10-ounce) jar grape jelly

Preheat the oven to 400°F.

Line a sheet pan with parchment paper and set aside.

To make the meatballs, in a large bowl, combine the sirloin, bread crumbs, onion, milk, egg, parsley, Worcestershire sauce, salt, and pepper with your fingertips. Be careful not to overwork the mixture. Gently form 1-inch meatballs and place on the prepared sheet pan. Bake until browned and cooked through, about 20 minutes.

Meanwhile, to make the sauce, combine the chili sauce and grape jelly in a small saucepan and stir together over medium heat until combined and heated through.

Remove the meatballs from the oven and toss to coat with the sauce. Transfer to a large serving platter. Or, if you're feeling truly nostalgic for that retro charm, keep warm in a Crock-Pot. Serve with plenty of toothpicks.

Prosciutto-Wrapped Grilled Plums serves 8
with Gorgonzola and Rosemary

Whenever my friends attend parties I can hardly wait to corner them and find out all about the food that was served. Forget the guest list or the locale. I want to know about the food! A good friend of mine recently attended a very chic wedding in Malibu and couldn't wait to tell me all about these little bites. Grilled plum with a bit of crumbly Gorgonzola slightly melted on the top, wrapped up in buttery pro-sciutto and fastened together with a sprig of rosemary. An elegant, easy starter

2   purple or black plums, pitted and sliced into eighths

Extra-virgin olive oil, for brushing plums

8   teaspoons Gorgonzola cheese, crumbled or sliced

8   slices prosciutto

16   small sprigs fresh rosemary

Preheat a grill pan or outdoor grill over high heat.

Lightly brush the plum slices with the oil and place on the hot grill, being careful to keep them from falling through the grate. Turn once to get grill marks on each cut side of the fruit. Remove and cool slightly. Place 1/2 teaspoon Gorgonzola on each slice of plum. Cut each slice of prosciutto in half lengthwise. Wrap the prosciutto around each plum slice and skewer with a sprig of rosemary to secure.

Stuffed Mushrooms

makes 24 mushrooms

I had these mushrooms years ago at a party and asked the hostess for the recipe. She happily scrawled it out on the back of a grocery receipt where it's remained ever since, until now. These mushrooms are always a hit, so make plenty.

24   white or cremini mushrooms, cleaned with a damp cloth

1/2   white onion

2   tablespoons unsalted butter

3   tablespoons all-purpose flour

1/2   cup heavy cream

    Kosher salt and freshly cracked black pepper, to taste

    Swiss cheese, grated, for topping

Preheat the oven to 375°F.

Clean the mushroom caps with a damp cloth and carefully remove the stems; set caps aside. Mince the stems and the onion in a food processor.

Melt the butter in a medium sauté pan over medium heat and cook the mushroom stems and onions until tender, about 5 minutes. Add the flour and cook 1 more minute to remove the raw taste. Whisk in the cream and bring to a bubble. Cook until thickened, 1 to 2 minutes. Season with salt and pepper. Using a small spoon, fill the cavity of each mushroom cap with the mixture, slightly mounding on top. Place mushrooms on a sheet pan. Sprinkle with grated cheese and bake, uncovered, until mushrooms are tender and the stuffing is heated through, about 20 minutes.

Asian Beef Lettuce Wraps serves 4

1 1/3   pounds ground sirloin

2   cloves garlic, minced

1   (1-inch) piece of ginger, peeled and minced

1   jalapeño pepper, seeded and diced

Grated zest and freshly squeezed juice of 1 lime

2   tablespoons tamari (dark soy sauce)

1   scant tablespoon fish sauce (nam pla or nuoc mam)*

1   to 2 teaspoons sambal oelek (Asian hot chili paste), or to taste

1   (8-ounce) can water chestnuts, drained and thinly sliced

2   tablespoons finely chopped fresh mint

2   tablespoons finely chopped cilantro

3   scallions, thinly sliced

2   heads butter or iceberg lettuce, leaves separated

1/2   seedless cucumber, julienned, for garnish

Try as I might, I tend not to stick to any particular diet theory for more than a few weeks at a time (I'm weak, what can I say?). I first came across lettuce wraps while on a low-carb kick a few years back. Using cool, crisp leaves of lettuce to surround a warm, spicy meat filling provides the perfect contrast in texture and temperature. Now it doesn't matter whether I'm on the dietary straight and narrow, I eat these every chance I get! They're great as an appetizer or a very satisfying meal on their own.

In a medium sauté pan, brown the meat over medium heat, stirring occasionally to break it up. Add the garlic, ginger, and jalapeño. Stir occasionally until the meat is no longer pink; drain if necessary. Add the lime zest, lime juice, tamari, fish sauce, sambal, water chestnuts, mint, and cilantro. Stir to combine, and turn the ground meat out onto a serving platter. Scatter with scallions. To eat, spoon the filling into the lettuce leaves and garnish with cucumber.

Fish sauce can be found in Asian markets in most cities. Some major markets carry it on the Asian aisle.

Vietnamese Spring Rolls with Sweet and Spicy Dipping Sauce

makes 20 rolls

FOR THE SPRING ROLLS

2 tablespoons sesame seeds

Kosher salt and freshly cracked black pepper, to taste

1/2 pound peeled and deveined shrimp

1 cup grated carrots

1 cup bean sprouts

2 cups finely shredded Napa cabbage

1/2 cup chopped basil

1/2 cup chopped cilantro

1/2 cup chopped mint leaves

1/2 hothouse cucumber, seeded and grated

20 (12-inch) rice paper wrappers*

FOR THE DIPPING SAUCE

2 tablespoons minced shallots

2 tablespoons tamari (dark soy sauce)

1 tablespoon fish sauce (nam pla or nuoc mam)*

2 tablespoons freshly squeezed lime juice

1 tablespoon dark brown sugar

1 red Thai chile or red jalapeño, chopped, with seeds (omit seeds for a milder sauce)

Start the spring rolls: Place the sesame seeds in a dry sauté pan and push them around over medium heat until they begin to deepen in color and their nutty aroma begins to waft up under your nose.

Put a large pot of water on to boil. Generously salt the water after it comes to a boil and add the shrimp; cook just until they are opaque, pink, and curled in on themselves, 2 to 3 minutes. Drain and allow them to cool completely. To speed up the cooling process, plunge them straight into a bowl of ice water for 1 to 2 minutes. When the shrimp have cooled, chop them finely.

Meanwhile, make the dipping sauce: In a small serving bowl, combine the shallots, tamari, fish sauce, lime juice, brown sugar, and chopped chile.

In a large bowl combine the shrimp, carrots, bean sprouts, Napa cabbage, basil, cilantro, mint, cucumber, and sesame seeds. Toss to combine and season with salt and pepper.

These spring rolls are so cool to make for a party! They're really easy to put together once you get the hang of working with the rice paper. And they are the kind of chic, impressive offering that will dazzle your guests (assuming you care about such things) because they look complicated. But the only complicated thing is figuring out how many to make.

Fill a pie plate with hot tap water and soak a single rice paper wrapper until it becomes transparent and pliable, about 30 seconds. It will go from stiff and brittle to "jelly-like" in a matter of seconds. Drain briefly as you lift it from the water and lay flat on a work surface. Place a small handful of the filling, about 2 tablespoons, off-center toward the bottom third of the circle and wrap up tightly like a burrito (fold up the bottom, fold in the sides, and roll up). This takes a little practice and the rice paper may tear, but after one or two tries it will come to you. If it's a complete disaster, return the filling to the bowl and start over with a new wrapper. Repeat with remaining rice paper and filling. Place each spring roll under a layer of damp paper towels to keep until you're ready to serve.

These can be made up to 1 day ahead and stored in the refrigerator covered tightly with a damp paper towel and plastic wrap. Slice the spring rolls on an angle and serve with dipping sauce.

Rice paper wrappers and fish sauce can be found in Asian markets in most cities. Some major markets carry them on the Asian aisle.

Brie, Mango, and Mint Wraps with Lime-Cream Dipping Sauce

serves 4

I developed this recipe when I screen-tested for a cooking show pilot that required making an appetizer in ten minutes or less, without using heat. It happened to be one of the hottest days of the year and I was a nervous wreck! With the cameras rolling, I began to slice the mango. At the same time, I had to talk to the camera, be engaging, and keep the segment moving. Without realizing it, I nicked my finger and started bleeding all over the cutting board. My co-host shrieked, the director yelled, "Cut!" and I didn't get the job. This recipe is the one good thing that came from that experience. I love to serve it in summer when mangoes are at their peak.

FOR THE DIPPING SAUCE

- 1 cup sour cream
- 2 tablespoons sugar
- 1 tablespoon freshly squeezed lime juice
- 2 teaspoons grated lime zest

FOR THE WRAPS

- 2 ripe mangos, peeled, pitted, and thinly sliced
- 2 sheets lavosh flat bread
- 3/4 pound brie cheese, rind removed, thinly sliced
- 2 tablespoons chopped fresh mint leaves

To make the sauce, in a small bowl, stir together the sour cream, sugar, lime juice, and lime zest. Cover and refrigerate for at least 30 minutes to allow flavors to develop.

To make the wraps, place the sliced mango over the entire surface of the lavosh, repeat with the brie. Lightly dribble some of the sauce over the entire surface of the wrap and sprinkle with the mint. Starting at one of the long ends, tightly roll the lavosh jelly-roll fashion, and slice into 1-inch sections to make pinwheels. Serve cut-side up with remaining dipping sauce on the side.

Pan-Seared Filet Mignon with Horseradish Cream

serves 10

If you decide to make this for a party, take my advice and make plenty. They never fail to steal the show.

1 French baguette, sliced thin on an angle

2 tablespoons extra-virgin olive oil, plus more for brushing bread

Kosher salt and freshly cracked black pepper

2 (8-ounce) filet mignon steaks

1 cup sour cream

1/4 cup prepared horseradish

1 bag pre-washed baby arugula

2 tablespoons chopped chives, for garnish

Preheat the oven to 400°F.

Brush one side of each baguette slice lightly with oil. Season with salt and pepper to taste. Place on a baking sheet and bake until lightly brown and crisp, 4 to 5 minutes. Set aside.

Pat the steaks dry with a paper towel and season generously with salt and pepper. In a heavy, ovenproof skillet over medium-high heat, heat 2 tablespoons oil until almost smoking. Sear the steaks, on one side only, until the meat begins to caramelize, about 2 minutes. Resist the urge to touch or poke at the meat so that caramelization can occur. Without flipping the steak, transfer the pan to the oven and roast for about 10 minutes for medium-rare (a meat thermometer should register 130° to 140°F). Allow the meat to rest, loosely tented under a piece of aluminum foil, for 10 minutes to allow the juices to redistribute. Slice into 1/4-inch strips.

Meanwhile, in a small bowl, combine the sour cream and horseradish. Season with salt and pepper. Place a dollop of the horseradish sauce on each slice of bread along with one or two of the baby arugula leaves. Top with a slice of the filet and another small dollop of the horseradish cream; sprinkle with chives. Serve immediately.

Mixed Green Salad

with Candied Walnuts, Gorgonzola, and Pears

FOR THE CANDIED WALNUTS

1/2   cup sugar

2   tablespoons water

1/4   teaspoon pure vanilla extract

1   cup walnut halves

FOR THE VINAIGRETTE

1   tablespoon minced shallots

1   tablespoon good Dijon mustard

1/4   cup champagne vinegar

1/2   cup extra-virgin olive oil

    Kosher salt and freshly cracked black pepper, to taste

FOR THE SALAD

1   pear

    Freshly squeezed lemon juice, for pear

1   bag of pre-washed mixed baby greens

1/4   cup Gorgonzola cheese, crumbled

I wish I could take credit for this flavor combination, but it's one that I've tried to re-create from memory. I had this salad at a little bistro, as a starter to my meal, and I was intrigued. It has since become one of the most requested things I make for friends and clients. The pungent sharp Gorgonzola contrasts perfectly with the delicate pears and the sweet crunch of the candied walnuts. Think of this as salad with an edge.

To make the candied walnuts, line a cookie sheet with parchment paper. In a medium saucepan over high heat, bring the sugar and water to a boil; boil for 1 minute. Stir in the vanilla and walnut halves; stir until coating sets. Spread on the prepared cookie sheet and cool completely. Break apart if necessary.

To make the vinaigrette, in a small bowl, whisk together the shallots, mustard, and vinegar. Slowly drizzle in the oil, whisking constantly to emulsify. Season with salt and pepper.

To make the salad, slice the pear in half lengthwise, scoop out the core with a melon baller. Cut the halves lengthwise into quarters and then each quarter into 4 thin slices; toss the pear slices with a little lemon juice.

Place a good handful of greens on each plate. Top each with about 4 tablespoons candied walnuts and the Gorgonzola cheese, and finish with 4 pear slices, fanned like a peacock tail over the top. Drizzle with the vinaigrette.

Iceberg Wedges with Real Thousand Island Dressing

serves 4

FOR THE DRESSING

1	cup mayonnaise
1/4	cup ketchup
2	tablespoons white vinegar
2	teaspoons sugar
3	tablespoons sweet pickle relish
1	teaspoon minced white onion
	Kosher salt and freshly cracked black pepper, to taste

FOR THE SALAD

1	large head iceberg lettuce
1/2	cup cooked and crumbled bacon
4	plum tomatoes, seeded and finely diced
4	hard-boiled eggs
1/2	cup chopped fresh flat-leaf parsley, for garnish

There was a time in my life, I'm not proud to say, when I thought iceberg was the only type of lettuce on the planet. Once I discovered the truth, it was a revelation—I turned my back on iceberg completely. I treated it like the ugly stepchild of the salad world. Well, I'm happy to report that I've seen the error of my ways. Iceberg may not be the most glamorous leaf in the bowl, but I do think it's underrated. After all, none of those designer lettuces possess the same crunch or hold up to thick, creamy dressings the way iceberg does. For this recipe, nothing else will do.

To make the dressing, in a small bowl, mix together the mayonnaise, ketchup, vinegar, sugar, sweet pickle relish, and onion; season with salt and pepper. Cover and place in the refrigerator for a few hours to allow the flavors to develop. The longer, the better!

To assemble the salad, cut the core out of the lettuce and slice the head into 4 wedges. Place each wedge on a plate and drizzle with the dressing. Sprinkle with the crumbled bacon and diced tomatoes. Grate one egg over each wedge and shower with a small handful of chopped parsley.

Warm Spinach Salad with Red Grapes and Pancetta

serves 6

FOR THE DRESSING

3 tablespoons balsamic vinegar

1/4 cup extra-virgin olive oil

1/4 teaspoon kosher salt

1/4 teaspoon freshly cracked black pepper

FOR THE SALAD

1 pound baby spinach leaves, cleaned and drained

1/2 cup cubed pancetta

1/4 cup raw pine nuts

1/2 cup thinly sliced red onion

1 cup halved seedless red grapes

1 cup freshly grated Parmesan cheese

This is a swankier, more grown-up version of My Favorite Spinach Salad with Bacon (page 155). With Italian pancetta, pine nuts, and red grapes, it's fit for company. The only thing to remember here, and it's not a big deal, is that the salad must be tossed with the warm dressing at the absolute last minute before serving, since the heat will slightly wilt the spinach leaves. This salad waits for no one. That said, the dressing only takes a few minutes to put together and the ingredients for it can be prepped, assembled, and ready to go in advance.

To make the dressing, in a small bowl, whisk together the vinegar and oil; season with salt and pepper.

To make the salad, place the spinach in a large bowl. Cook the pancetta in a medium sauté pan over medium heat until just starting to crisp. Remove the pancetta from the pan with a slotted spoon and drain on a paper towel; don't drain the fat from the pan. Add the pine nuts and cook until they begin to toast, about 1 minute. Add the onion and grapes to the pan, cook 1 minute more. Pour the dressing into the pan and a boil for 30 seconds. Remove from heat and pour over the spinach. Toss well, sprinkle with Parmesan cheese, and serve immediately.

Oven-Roasted Salsa

makes about 3 cups

There is a famous Mexican-restaurant chain that turns out semi-decent food, but their salsa is to die for! And I don't even like salsa that much. What makes theirs stand out is the deep smoky flavor, which comes from roasting the tomatoes and onions, and from the addition of Liquid Smoke. I made a few attempts before I finally got it right. I think this is pretty close. Try it with Baja-Style Fried Fish Tacos (page 106).

6	large tomatoes
1	medium red onion
6	cloves garlic
1	jalapeño pepper, seeded and finely chopped
1	tablespoon coarsely chopped fresh cilantro
2	teaspoons sugar
1	teaspoon Liquid Smoke
1	teaspoon freshly cracked black pepper
2	green chile peppers, Anaheim or California

Preheat the broiler.

In a food processor, coarsely chop 3 of the tomatoes. Add 1/2 of the red onion, the garlic, jalapeño, cilantro, sugar, Liquid Smoke, and black pepper. Process until everything is coarsely chopped. Pour the mixture into a medium bowl.

Cut the remaining 3 tomatoes in half and place on a sheet pan with the remaining 1/2 red onion and the green chiles. Broil until everything gets very dark with brownish black spots on them, about 5 to 10 minutes. Keep a close eye on the oven and rotate the pan, if necessary, to ensure even browning. Remove from the oven and coarsely process in the food processor, skin and all. Combine both mixtures and chill for 4 to 6 hours to allow the flavors to develop.

Prosciutto-Wrapped Asparagus

serves 12

Kosher salt and freshly cracked black pepper, to taste

36   stalks asparagus

18   slices prosciutto

2/3   cup vegetable oil

1/4   cup balsamic vinegar

2   tablespoons good Dijon mustard

If the whole idea of wrapping up cutesy little bundles of food sounds terribly fussy to you, I can assure you, this isn't that pretentious "pinkies-up" kind of food that will make you think you've flashed back to the '80s. But, there is something to be said for the saltiness of the prosciutto against the blandness of the asparagus. The whole thing dipped in the sweet balsamic sauce will make it well worth any raised eyebrows you may get from your friends. They'll forgive you once they've tasted it.

Bring a large pot of water to a boil and generously season with salt. Meanwhile, fill a large bowl with ice water and push a colander or mesh strainer down into the water. Plunge the asparagus into the boiling water and cook until just blanched—bright green and still crisp—45 seconds to 1 minute, depending on the thickness of the spears. Remove the asparagus from the boiling water and immediately plunge them into the ice bath. Drain well.

Cut each piece of prosciutto in half lengthwise and wrap one piece around each stalk of asparagus.

In a small bowl whisk together the oil, vinegar, and mustard; season with salt and pepper. Just before serving, drizzle the dressing over the asparagus. Serve the rest on the side for dipping.

Crispy Calamari with Orange-Ginger Dipping Sauce

serves 4

I can never resist the temptation of calamari on any appetizer menu. Even if I'm not that hungry, which isn't often, I just have to have it! My favorite version is this tempura-like recipe that, like the Banana Fritters (page 160), is made with ice-cold seltzer water, resulting in a crispy coating that simply won't lose its crunch. I can't pretend that battering the calamari rings a few at a time isn't a bit tedious, but the result is well worth it.

FOR THE DIPPING SAUCE

1	tablespoon extra-virgin olive oil
1	tablespoon minced fresh ginger
1	teaspoon minced shallot
1/2	teaspoon dried red chile flakes
1	cup freshly squeezed orange juice
	Grated zest of 1 orange
1/2	cup orange marmalade
1	teaspoon chopped fresh cilantro
1	teaspoon chopped fresh mint
1	teaspoon chopped fresh basil

FOR THE CALAMARI

	Canola oil, for frying
1	cup all-purpose flour
1	cup cornstarch
2	teaspoons kosher salt
2	teaspoons freshly cracked black pepper
1	teaspoon cayenne pepper, or to taste
1 1/4	cups ice-cold seltzer water
1	pound calamari, cleaned and cut into 1/2-inch rings
	Lemon wedges, for garnish

To make the dipping sauce, heat the oil in a medium sauté pan over medium heat and sauté the ginger, shallot, and chile flakes until fragrant and softened, about 2 minutes. Add the orange juice and zest, increase the heat to high and reduce liquid by half, about 3 minutes. Add the orange marmalade and simmer over low heat for another minute. Remove from heat and stir in the cilantro, mint, and basil. Set aside to cool.

To make the calamari, fill a heavy-bottom frying pan or Dutch oven with 2 inches canola oil. Heat the oil over high heat to 375°F on a deep-fry thermometer.

Meanwhile, in a large bowl, whisk together the flour, cornstarch, salt, black pepper, and cayenne pepper. Slowly whisk in the seltzer water. The batter will be slightly lumpy and resemble pancake batter.

Dip the calamari rings in the batter, a few pieces at a time, shaking off the excess, and gently slide them into the oil, being careful not to overcrowd the pan. Fry until golden brown, about 2 minutes, adjusting heat to maintain oil temperature. Remove to a paper towel-lined platter using a slotted spoon or Chinese strainer. Continue until all calamari are fried. Spritz with lemon juice and serve with dipping sauce. Gorgeous!

Real Maryland Crab Cakes with Creamy Herb Remoulade

FOR THE SAUCE

- 1/2   cup mayonnaise
- 1/2   cup sour cream
- 1   tablespoon finely chopped fresh flat-leaf parsley
- 1   tablespoon finely chopped fresh dill

     Freshly squeezed juice of 1/2 lemon

     Kosher salt and freshly cracked black pepper, to taste

FOR THE CRAB CAKES

- 1   pound fresh lump crabmeat
- 1   large egg, lightly beaten
- 2 1/2   tablespoons mayonnaise
- 2   teaspoons freshly squeezed lemon juice
- 1 1/2   teaspoons Worcestershire sauce

     Several dashes hot sauce, or to taste

- 5   Saltine crackers, finely crushed
- 2   scallions, chopped
- 1   tablespoon chopped fresh flat-leaf parsley

     Freshly cracked black pepper

- 3   tablespoons vegetable oil

     Lemon wedges, for garnish

If you ask ten different crab cake lovers what makes a good crab cake, I can almost guarantee you'll get ten different opinions. Personally, I think it starts with really good, really fresh crabmeat. That may sound obvious, but you'd be surprised at how many people overlook that little detail. I also think it's a matter of using as few fillers as possible in order to showcase the star ingredient. I serve these dressed simply, with just a touch of herb remoulade sauce on the side.

To make the sauce, combine the mayonnaise, sour cream, parsley, dill, and lemon juice in a small bowl and season with salt and pepper. Set aside.

To make the crab cakes, place the crabmeat in a large bowl and pick through, making sure there are no shells. In another small bowl, whisk together the egg, mayonnaise, lemon juice, Worcestershire sauce, and hot sauce. Add the egg mixture to the crabmeat, along with the cracker crumbs, scallions, parsley, and pepper. I don't suggest extra salt because the crackers themselves are salted. Gently combine, being careful not to overwork; the mixture will be wet. With your hands, form the meat into 4 cakes of equal size.

Heat the oil in a large sauté pan over medium-high heat and gently slide the crab cakes into the pan. Pan-fry until the cakes are golden brown and cooked through, about 5 minutes per side. Serve warm with the herb remoulade sauce and lemon wedges.

42   BOY EATS WORLD!

Chicken Satay with Spicy Peanut Dipping Sauce

For the Chicken

- 1/2 cup coconut milk
- 1 tablespoon fish sauce (nam pla or nuoc mam)*
- 2 tablespoons freshly squeezed lime juice
- 2 teaspoons sambal oelek (Asian hot chili paste)
- 1 teaspoon dark brown sugar
- 1 tablespoon chopped fresh cilantro
- 2 tablespoons finely grated, peeled fresh ginger
- 1/2 teaspoon ground turmeric
   Kosher salt and freshly cracked black pepper
- 1 pound chicken tenders
   Bamboo skewers, soaked in water

For the Dipping Sauce

- 1 cup smooth natural peanut butter, well stirred
- 1/2 cup chicken stock
- 1/4 cup unseasoned rice vinegar
- 3 tablespoons dark brown sugar
- 2 tablespoons tamari (dark soy sauce)
- 2 tablespoons grated, peeled fresh ginger
- 2 teaspoons sambal oelek (Asian hot chili paste)
- 1 teaspoon turmeric
- 1 tablespoon chopped dry-roasted unsalted peanuts

Chicken satay is hardly new and exciting fare these days. But it is one of the first things to go at a party! For that reason alone, it is a good thing to have in your culinary repertoire.

To make the chicken, in a medium bowl combine the coconut milk, fish sauce, lime juice, sambal, brown sugar, cilantro, ginger, and turmeric, and season with salt and pepper. Place the chicken tenders in a heavy, gallon-size resealable plastic bag. Add the marinade. Marinate at room temperature for 30 minutes or for several hours in the refrigerator. The longer the meat swims in the marinade, the more flavorful it will be.

Meanwhile, to make the sauce, in a medium saucepan, whisk together the peanut butter, chicken stock, rice vinegar, brown sugar, tamari, ginger, sambal, and turmeric. Heat gently over medium heat. Cool, then garnish with chopped peanuts.

Preheat an indoor grill pan or outdoor grill to high.

Thread the chicken tenders onto the bamboo skewers and grill until chicken is cooked through, about 2 to 3 minutes per side. Serve immediately with spicy peanut dipping sauce.

*Fish sauce can be found in Asian markets in most cities. Some major markets carry it on the Asian aisle.

Black Bean and Corn Salsa

serves 4

I'm not much of a sports fan. But that doesn't stop me from throwing a big party on Super Bowl Sunday, if for no other reason than to get everyone together and make lots of great picking food. This salsa scores a home run every time. Or is it a touchdown?

1   (15-ounce) can black beans, drained and rinsed

1   (15-ounce) can corn, drained

1/4   cup chopped cilantro

2   cloves garlic, minced

2   tablespoons freshly squeezed lime juice

1   tablespoon honey

1   teaspoon ground cumin

1   teaspoon hot sauce, or to taste

1   teaspoon unseasoned rice wine vinegar

    Kosher salt and freshly cracked black pepper, to taste

In a medium bowl, combine the beans, corn, cilantro, garlic, lime juice, honey, cumin, hot sauce, rice wine vinegar, salt, and pepper. Stir gently to combine, and refrigerate for several hours to let the flavors marry. Serve with tortilla chips and your favorite beer in frosted mugs.

Easy Hummus

makes 3 cups

A Lebanese friend of mine introduced me to the idea of serving hummus sprinkled with fresh pomegranate seeds, as is traditional in Lebanon. It's delicious, but not always practical. When pomegranates aren't available, I opt for toasted pine nuts and a drizzle of extra-virgin olive oil instead. Serve with fresh vegetables and/or Middle Eastern Flat Bread (page 123).

2	(15-ounce) cans chickpeas
1/3	cup freshly squeezed lemon juice
1/2	cup tahini*, well stirred
4	cloves garlic, chopped
	Pinch of cayenne pepper, or to taste
	Kosher salt, to taste
1/4	cup extra-virgin olive oil, plus more for drizzling
1/4	cup fresh pomegranate seeds, for garnish
	Or
1/4	cup pine nuts, toasted**, for garnish

Drain the chickpeas, reserving 1/4 cup liquid; rinse. Place the chickpeas in the bowl of a food processor along with the reserved liquid, lemon juice, tahini, garlic, cayenne pepper, salt, and oil. Blitz together until smooth, scraping down the sides as necessary. Transfer to a serving bowl and drizzle with oil and sprinkle with pomegranate seeds or toasted pine nuts.

Tahini is a thick paste (think peanut butter) made from 100% crushed sesame seeds. It is a key ingredient in hummus, the traditional Middle Eastern chickpea spread.

**Place pine nuts in a dry sauté pan over medium heat and push them around until they begin to deepen in color and their nutty aroma begins to waft up under your nose. Remove from heat.*

Wild Mushroom Strudel

serves 6 to 8

1¼   pounds assorted wild
      mushrooms (shiitake, oyster,
      cremini, enoki)

2   tablespoons extra-virgin olive oil

8   tablespoons unsalted butter

2   cloves garlic, minced

1   shallot, minced

2   tablespoons good, dry white
      wine

1   teaspoon finely chopped fresh
      rosemary

1   teaspoon finely chopped fresh
      thyme

1/2   cup heavy cream
      Kosher salt and freshly cracked
      black pepper, to taste

8   sheets (9x13) frozen phyllo
      dough, thawed

If the idea of working with phyllo dough freaks you out or intimidates you, all I can say is, get over it! There are far more reasons to use it than not. It's readily available in any large grocery store. It lasts for months in the freezer and has such a wide range of applications, from dinner to dessert, that it only makes sense that you become fast friends.

Preheat the oven to 400°F.

Remove woody stems from the shiitake mushrooms, if using, and discard. In a food processor or by hand, finely chop the mushrooms and set aside.

Heat the oil and 1 tablespoon of the butter in a large sauté pan over medium-low heat. Sauté the garlic and shallot until tender, 6 to 7 minutes. Add the mushrooms and increase the heat to medium-high; sauté the mushrooms until tender and they throw off their juice, about 10 minutes. Add the white wine to the pan to deglaze, scraping up any browned bits off the bottom of the pan. Cook to reduce juices until the pan is almost dry. Add the rosemary, thyme, and cream. Season with salt and pepper and reduce cream until thickened and almost dry. Remove from heat and cool the mushrooms to room temperature.

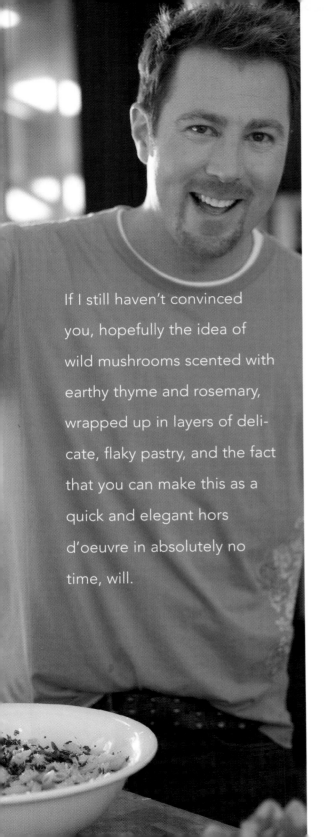

If I still haven't convinced you, hopefully the idea of wild mushrooms scented with earthy thyme and rosemary, wrapped up in layers of delicate, flaky pastry, and the fact that you can make this as a quick and elegant hors d'oeuvre in absolutely no time, will.

Line a sheet pan with parchment paper. In a small saucepan or in the microwave, melt the remaining 7 tablespoons butter. Place one sheet of phyllo dough on a work surface. Keep the remaining dough under a damp (not wet) towel to prevent drying out. Brush the phyllo with some of the melted butter and top with another layer of phyllo dough. Continue until you have 4 layers of dough. Don't be surprised if it looks a little ragged and the edges don't match up perfectly. All of that will be smoothed out when you roll the strudel. Spoon half of the mushroom mixture along the short side of the phyllo. Fold in the ends and roll up jelly-roll fashion, or like a burrito. Place the strudel seam side down on prepared sheet pan. Brush with butter and lightly score the strudel diagonally to make 8 equal pieces. Repeat with remaining phyllo dough and filling to make the second strudel. Bake until golden brown, 20 to 25 minutes. Allow the strudel to cool for about 15 minutes and serve sliced on an angle.

Ham and Fontina Mini-Frittatas

makes 24

These are my answer to those frozen miniature quiches that are always the first thing to go at any party. I love that you can whip up several in mere minutes, they're perfectly bite-sized, and they can be made a day ahead and gently reheated before serving.

Nonstick butter-flavored cooking spray, for muffin pan

1/4   pound smoked deli ham, finely chopped

1/4   cup Fontina cheese, finely grated

3   tablespoons fresh chives, chopped

8   large eggs

2   tablespoons heavy cream

        Kosher salt and freshly cracked black pepper

Preheat the oven to 375°F.

Lightly spray a mini-muffin pan(s) with nonstick cooking spray. In a small bowl, lightly toss together the ham, cheese, and chives. Evenly fill each muffin cup with the ham and cheese mixture. In a 4-cup measuring cup, whisk together the eggs and cream and season with salt and pepper. Pour the egg mixture into each cup until just even with the rim. Bake until frittatas are puffed and set, 10 to 12 minutes. Serve warm or at room temperature*.

*To reheat, place frittatas on a parchment-lined sheet pan and heat in a 325°F oven for about 5 minutes.

Caramelized Onion Tartlets

makes 24

This savory little party offering takes its cues from the classic caramelized French Onion Tart. The little tart shells are also great for dessert offerings. Just fill with fresh fruit or berries and top with a dollop of fresh whipped cream and a sprig of mint.

FOR THE TART SHELLS

1/4	cup unsalted butter, melted
1	loaf good white sandwich bread (Sara Lee or Pepperidge Farms brand)

FOR THE FILLING

6	tablespoons extra-virgin olive oil
4	medium onions, thinly sliced
2	bay leaves
1 1/2	teaspoons fresh thyme, chopped
	Kosher salt and freshly ground black pepper, to taste
1/2	cup grated Gruyère cheese, for topping

Preheat the oven to 350°F.

To make the tart shells, brush the inside of a mini-muffin pan(s) with the melted butter and set aside. Using a 3-inch round cookie cutter or an inverted drinking glass of the same size, cut a circle from the center of each piece of bread. Discard scraps or save for another use. With a rolling pin, flatten each bread round and place inside of each muffin cup. Brush with remaining butter and bake until lightly golden brown, 12 to 14 minutes. Remove from oven and allow to cool in the pan.

To make the filling, in a large skillet, heat olive oil over low heat. Add the onions, bay leaves, and thyme. Cook, stirring frequently, until soft and deep golden brown, 15 to 20 minutes. Don't rush this part, it takes a while for the onions to caramelize. The key to success is low and slow. When the onions are almost done, season with salt and pepper. Discard bay leaves.

Preheat the broiler to high.

To assemble the tartlets, fill each with some of the caramelized onion mixture and top with the grated cheese. Place under the broiler for a minute or so to melt the cheese and heat through. Serve immediately.

Figs with Goat Cheese and Port Syrup

serves 4

I came to appreciate figs relatively late in life. To be honest I didn't even know what a fresh fig looked like until my mid-20s. I have definitely made up for lost time, because I'm obsessed with them now. I love the simplicity of this recipe; the figs can be served as a starter or as an elegant finish to any meal.

1/2 cup walnuts

1 cup ruby port

6 tablespoons honey

6 ounces soft goat cheese (Montrachet)

8 ripe figs

2 tablespoons lightly chopped fresh flat-leaf parsley, for garnish

Place the walnuts in a dry sauté pan over medium heat and push them around until they deepen in color and their nutty aroma wafts up under your nose. Remove from heat and set aside to cool.

In a small saucepan, over medium-high heat, bring the port and honey to a boil. Reduce heat and simmer slowly until reduced by half. Set aside and cool to room temperature; the syrup will thicken considerably upon standing.

Cut the goat cheese into 8 equal pieces, about 2 teaspoons each, and roll each piece into a ball. Place the figs upright on a cutting board and carefully make four cross-cuts, being careful not to go all the way through the bottom, slicing each fig into eight sections. Gently separate the figs outward to form a "flower." Place a ball of goat cheese in the center of each fig and drizzle with the port syrup. Chop the walnuts and sprinkle over the figs; garnish with chopped parsley.

Mini-Cheeseburgers

Believe me, I'm happy with cheese-burgers of any size, but there's something charming about them in miniature. These babies certainly don't disappoint. The use of ready-made refrigerator dough, and the make ahead advantage, make them just the thing for a cocktail or kids' party.

makes 24

FOR THE SPECIAL SAUCE

- 1/4 cup good quality mayonnaise
- 1/4 cup ketchup

  Kosher salt and freshly cracked pepper, to taste

FOR THE BUNS

- 2 (11-ounce) packages refrigerated crusty French bread dough (Pillsbury brand)
- 1 large egg yolk plus one table-spoon water lightly beaten, for egg wash
- 2 tablespoons sesame seeds

FOR THE BURGERS

- 2 to 3 tablespoons extra-virgin olive oil, for pan searing
- 2 large egg yolks, lightly beaten
- 2 tablespoons A.1. steak sauce
- 1 1/2 tablespoons grill seasoning blend
- 1 1/2 pounds ground sirloin
- 6 slices deli-style sharp cheddar cheese, each cut into 4 equal squares
- 4 small plum tomatoes, thinly sliced

  Lettuce, torn to fit the burgers

Preheat the oven to 350°F.

To make the special sauce, in a small bowl, combine the mayonnaise, ketchup, salt, and pepper.

To make the buns, line a sheet pan with parchment paper and set aside. Cut each package of bread dough into 12 equal pieces. Roll each piece into a ball about the size of a golf ball, placing them on the prepared sheet pan as you finish them. Brush the buns with the egg wash and sprinkle with sesame seeds. Bake in the center of the oven until golden brown, 22 to 24 minutes. Remove to a rack and cool completely.

Meanwhile, to get started on the burgers, pre-heat olive oil in a medium skillet over medium-high heat until hot. In a medium bowl, whisk together the egg yolks, steak sauce, and grill seasoning. Add the ground sirloin and gently combine with your fingertips being careful not to overwork the meat. Using approximately 2 tablespoons of the meat mixture, carefully roll into meatballs and press between your palms to flatten into a small patty. Pan sear until cooked through to desired doneness, about 3 minutes on each side. Place a piece of cheese on each patty and tent loosely with a piece of foil to melt cheese.

To assemble the burgers, cut each bun in half crosswise and place a teaspoon-sized dollop of the special sauce on the bottom of each. Top with a hamburger patty, tomato slice, a piece of lettuce, and a bun top. Skewer each mini cheeseburger with a festive toothpick to hold together. Serve immediately.

Red-Pepper Jelly serves 6

6   large red bell peppers

1/2   teaspoon kosher salt

1   tablespoon unsalted butter

1 1/2   cups sugar

1   cup white vinegar

1   (8-ounce) brick cream cheese, room temperature, for serving

This pepper jelly is vibrant red and beautiful. It's perfect for the holidays. Granted, it does take some time to make, but it's nothing too strenuous. Just simmer over low heat and stir occasionally. Trust me, it's well worth the effort.

In a food processor, finely grind the peppers and transfer to a small bowl; sprinkle with salt. Let stand for 2 hours; the salt will help draw the liquid out of the peppers. Allow peppers to drain in a colander, removing as much liquid as possible, about 15 minutes. Discard liquid.

Melt the butter in a medium skillet over medium heat and add the peppers, sugar, and vinegar. Bring the mixture to a boil and immediately reduce heat to low. Simmer gently 2 hours, stirring occasionally. Cool to room temperature.

Place the brick of cream cheese on a serving platter. Spoon the pepper jelly generously over the cream cheese and serve with your favorite crackers.

Pistachio-Parmesan Truffles

makes 24

These bite-size morsels are a riff on the classic holiday cheese ball from back in the day. They've been updated here with Parmesan and pistachios, for a more elegant, contemporary presentation.

2   cups coarsely grated Parmesan cheese

1   cup ricotta cheese

    Kosher salt and freshly cracked black pepper, to taste

1   cup finely chopped unsalted pistachios

In a medium bowl, combine the Parmesan and ricotta and season with salt and pepper. Measure out one level teaspoon of the cheese mixture and roll into a ball. Repeat with remaining mixture. Roll truffles in the pistachios and refrigerate until ready to serve.

Tomato-Basil Bruschetta

serves 6

I don't remember where I was when I first tried bruschetta, but I remember thinking it was incredible! It seemed so worldly and sophisticated to me at the time. Well, the flavors are sophisticated, but the preparation is a snap. This makes a great first course for dinner or an elegant hors d'oeuvre at a cocktail party.

8	medium plum tomatoes
10	basil leaves
1/4	cup extra-virgin olive oil, plus more for brushing bread
2	tablespoons balsamic vinegar
	Kosher salt and freshly cracked black pepper, to taste
1	French baguette
2	cloves garlic, for rubbing the bread

Seed the tomatoes by cutting each one in half, cradling it in your hand cut side down and gently squeezing the seeds out. Dice the tomatoes. Chiffonade the basil by stacking them flat, one on top of the other, rolling them lengthwise into a cigar shape. Starting at one end and working across, thinly slice the leaves into fine ribbons and give them a quick toss to separate.

In a medium bowl, mix together the tomatoes, basil, oil, and vinegar. Season with salt and pepper and set aside at room temperature for several hours to allow the flavors to develop.

Just before serving, heat a grill pan. Slice the baguette on an angle into 1/4-inch-thick slices, and brush both sides lightly with oil. Grill until marked and golden brown on both sides. Remove from the grill and rub the edges of each slice of bread with the garlic cloves. Place bread slices on a serving platter and top each with a generous spoonful of the tomato-basil mixture.

Souped Up

Soup makes an elegant starter to any meal, or it can be a meal in itself. I don't know why people don't make it more often. Is it because they think that it's too difficult? Too time consuming? Maybe they think soup is boring.

Most of the recipes in this chapter come together quickly and range from the everyday to the exotic. Nothing boring here, I promise. These recipes can take you from Greece to Thailand to France and back again without so much as packing a bag or renewing your passport.

Homemade Split Pea Soup

serves 6

Split pea soup is one of those things you either love or hate. There is no in between. As a card-carrying split pea soup lover, I've made no attempt to reinvent the wheel here. This classic doesn't stray far from tradition.

1	pound dried green split peas, picked over and rinsed
2	large smoked ham hocks
1	large onion, chopped
2	stalks celery, chopped
1	large carrot, peeled and chopped
4	cloves garlic, smashed
10	sprigs fresh flat-leaf parsley
4	sprigs fresh thyme
1	bay leaf
4	cups water
1	quart chicken stock
	Kosher salt and freshly cracked black pepper, to taste

In a Dutch oven or large, heavy-bottom stockpot, combine the peas, ham hocks, onion, celery, carrot, and garlic. Tie the parsley, thyme, and bay leaf together with kitchen twine. Add the herb bundle, water, and chicken stock to the pot and bring to a boil over high heat. Lower the heat to a gentle simmer, cover, and cook until the peas are tender, about 1 1/2 hours. Turn off the heat and remove the ham hocks. Allow them to cool completely. Remove the meat from the hocks, discarding the bones, fat, and skin. Cut the meat into cubes and set aside. Remove the herb bundle and discard.

Puree the soup with a handheld immersion blender, or in batches using a blender. Gently reheat the soup to a simmer, stir in the meat, and season with salt and pepper. Serve immediately.

Chilled Avocado Soup

If there's anything more sublime than a perfect summer day, it's this soup on a perfect summer day. It's cold and creamy and completely satisfying. I keep it in a pitcher in the fridge, next to the Ginger-Infused Lemonade (page 198), and pour it into big mugs to sip poolside. I ask you, does life get any better than this?

serves 6

Peel and dice the avocados and sprinkle with the lemon juice. In a blender combine the avocados, chicken stock, milk, and both creams; puree on low speed until completely smooth. Season with salt and white pepper. Refrigerate for several hours and serve well chilled.

Mexican cream can be found on the dairy aisle. If you can't find it, substitute heavy cream, which will result in a slightly thinner soup.

2	large, ripe Haas avocados
1	tablespoon freshly squeezed lemon juice
2	cups chicken stock
2	cups milk
2/3	cup sour cream
2/3	cup light Mexican cream*
	Kosher salt and white pepper, to taste

Steak and Red Wine Soup

serves 6

This is one of those great soups that has "all-day flavor," but comes together in no time at all. The wine adds sophistication and the beef stock adds depth of flavor. Serve this with a great crusty bread, and it's a meal all by itself.

1	tablespoon extra-virgin olive oil
1	pound New York strip steak (or rib-eye) cut into 1/2-inch chunks
	Freshly cracked black pepper
3	tablespoons unsalted butter
1/2	onion, chopped
2	carrots, peeled and chopped
2	stalks celery, chopped
1	bay leaf
1/4	cup all-purpose flour
3	(14-ounce) cans beef stock
1/2	cup good, dry red wine
1	(14-ounce) can diced tomatoes in their juice
2	teaspoons chopped fresh thyme

Heat the oil in a Dutch oven or large, heavy-bottom stockpot over high heat until almost smoking. Season the beef generously with pepper and cook for about 1 minute (turning only once) until seared on both sides. The meat should be caramelized but not overcooked; it will finish cooking in the soup. Remove from pot; set aside.

In the same pot, melt the butter and sauté the onions, carrots, celery, and bay leaf until the vegetables begin to soften, 2 to 3 minutes. Make a roux by adding the flour, stirring constantly, scraping up the brown bits on the bottom of the pot (lots of flavor here!), until the raw flavor has been cooked out of the flour, another 2 to 3 minutes. Stir in the stock, wine, tomatoes, and thyme. Bring to a boil. Reduce heat and simmer gently until the vegetables are tender, at least 15 minutes. Discard bay leaf.

Stir the beef and the drippings back into the soup. Cook about 2 more minutes for medium rare, or until desired doneness. Adjust the seasonings as needed and serve in large bowls.

Avgolemono
(Chicken Soup with Lemon and Egg Sauce)

When I was 17, I worked with a woman who told me this was one of the first Greek recipes she learned to cook for her Greek husband. Avgolemono, she explained, is traditionally served for Greek Easter. Not only did I think the name was bizarre, but the thought of lemon and egg in a soup seemed incomprehensible to me. Boy, was I wrong. I think of her every time I make this incredible soup.

3   pounds boneless, skinless chicken breasts

2   quarts chicken stock

2   bay leaves

1   leek, white part only, cleaned and quartered

1   carrot, peeled and quartered

2   tablespoons extra-virgin olive oil

1   onion, finely diced

2/3   cup arborio rice

2   large eggs

1/2   cup freshly squeezed lemon juice

1   teaspoon kosher salt

1   teaspoon freshly cracked black pepper

1   lemon, thinly sliced, for garnish

Place the chicken breasts in a large pot with the chicken stock, bay leaves, leek, and carrot. Bring to a boil and reduce heat to low; simmer gently until the chicken is just cooked through, 8 to 10 minutes.

Meanwhile, in a medium sauté pan over medium heat, heat the oil and add the onions. Sauté until translucent, about 6 minutes. Set aside.

When the chicken is done, remove from the stock and discard the bay leaves, leek, and carrot. Let the chicken cool, then dice it into large cubes. Add the rice to the stock and bring stock back to a boil; reduce heat and simmer until rice is cooked to al dente, about 30 minutes. Add the chicken back into the stock and heat through.

In a small bowl, beat the eggs and lemon juice together. Pour 2 cups of the chicken stock slowly into the bowl of egg and lemon, whisking constantly to temper. This step ensures that you won't scramble the eggs when you add them to the soup. Pour the tempered eggs into the pot and stir to blend throughout. Season with salt and pepper. Serve hot with a thin slice of lemon floating beautifully on the top.

Pasta e Fagioli

serves 6

The thing I love most about this classic soup, aside from the taste, is that it comes together so quickly with ingredients you probably have on hand. It's incredibly satisfying too—everything you need in one pot.

Kosher salt and freshly cracked black pepper

1/2 cup small macaroni

1 tablespoon extra-virgin olive oil

1 medium onion, chopped

4 cloves garlic, minced

2 stalks celery, diced

3/4 pound lean ground sirloin

2 medium carrots, grated

1 (10-ounce) jar Prego Traditional marinara sauce

1 (14-ounce) can diced tomatoes with their juice

1 (14-ounce) can kidney beans, drained and rinsed

1 (14-ounce) can cannelini beans, drained and rinsed

1 bay leaf

1 quart beef stock

Bring a large pot of water to a boil, then add a generous amount of salt. Add the macaroni and cook, according to package directions, to al dente.

Meanwhile, in a Dutch oven or large, heavy-bottom stockpot, heat the oil and sauté the onion, garlic, and celery until just soft, about 3 minutes. Add the ground sirloin; season generously with salt and pepper and cook until there's no pink left in the meat. Drain off any excess fat. Add the carrots, marinara sauce, tomatoes, beans, bay leaf, and beef stock. Bring to a boil, reduce heat, and simmer until the vegetables are tender and the flavors have time to develop, about 20 minutes. Stir in the cooked macaroni just before serving.

Cream of Macadamia Nut Soup serves 8

I'd never heard of it either, but after hearing a friend's friend at a party go on and on about Cream of Macadamia Nut Soup, I begged for the recipe. Several e-mails later, I had it! I couldn't wait to try it and once I did, the results were surprisingly delicious.

2   sticks unsalted butter, cut into pieces

2   carrots, peeled and chopped

1   leek, white part only, cleaned and chopped

2   stalks celery, chopped

1   clove garlic, minced

1   cup ground macadamia nuts, plus 1 cup chopped

2   tablespoons all-purpose flour

2   quarts chicken stock

2   bay leaves

1   cup heavy cream

    Kosher salt and white pepper, to taste

1/2   cup chopped fresh flat-leaf parsley, for garnish

In a Dutch oven or a large, heavy-bottom stockpot, melt one stick of butter and sauté the carrots, leek, celery, and garlic until tender. Add the ground macadamia nuts and cook another minute. Add the flour and cook for 2 minutes, stirring constantly to cook out the raw flavor. Whisk in the chicken stock and bay leaves. Bring to a boil then reduce heat and simmer gently for 1 hour.

Strain the soup through a fine-mesh sieve into a large saucepan. Cut the remaining stick of butter into little pieces and add to the strained stock along with the cream. Add the chopped nuts, holding some back for garnish. Season with salt and pepper. Heat the soup thoroughly, but do not bring back to a boil. Garnish with reserved chopped nuts and parsley.

Wild Mushroom and Barley Soup

serves 6

This soup bears a passing resemblance to the more delicate French Mushroom Soup (page 71), but is heartier with the addition of barley and deeply flavored, meaty porcinis. Although they can be difficult to find fresh, porcinis are easy to come by dried and can be brought back to life with a bit of hot water.

2 ounces dried porcini mushrooms

3 1/2 cups hot water

1/4 cup extra-virgin olive oil

1 medium onion, chopped

2 medium carrots, peeled and diced

2 stalks celery, diced

1 pound cremini mushrooms, cleaned with a damp cloth and sliced

2 teaspoons chopped fresh thyme

Kosher salt and freshly cracked black pepper, to taste

1 quart beef stock

1/2 cup barley

1/2 cup chopped fresh flat-leaf parsley

In a medium bowl, soak the porcini mushrooms in the hot water for 20 minutes.

Meanwhile, in a large stockpot or Dutch oven over medium heat, heat the oil and sauté the onion, carrots, and celery until softened, about 5 minutes. Add the cremini mushrooms and thyme. Cook until the mushrooms soften and give off their liquid, 5 or 6 minutes. Season with salt and pepper.

Fish the porcini mushrooms out of the soaking liquid with a slotted spoon and chop roughly. Strain the liquid through a fine-mesh sieve or a piece of cheesecloth to catch any grit that has collected on the bottom of the bowl. Add the porcini mushrooms and soaking liquid to the pot along with the beef stock and barley. Bring to a boil; reduce heat and simmer gently until the barley is tender, about 40 minutes. Stir in the parsley and serve immediately.

Thai-Inspired Lemongrass, Banana, and Coconut Soup

serves 4 to 6

1/4	cup extra-virgin olive oil
2	ripe bananas, sliced
1	small onion, chopped
3	cloves garlic, chopped
1	large leek, white and pale green part, thinly sliced
2	stalks celery, chopped
3/4	cup chopped carrot
1	stalk lemongrass, white part only, tough outer stalks removed, minced
1	teaspoon ground cumin
1/4	cup roughly chopped cilantro, plus more for garnish
1	cup freshly squeezed orange juice
2	(14-ounce) cans vegetable stock
1	(14-ounce) can unsweetened coconut milk

I don't know who came up with the unusual addition of bananas and coconut to a savory soup. But I'm eternally grateful for their culinary vision, as you will be, too, once you've tasted it. I promise these flavors go nowhere near piña colada territory. The end result is a soup that is silky, perfectly spiced, and utterly unexpected.

In a Dutch oven or large stock pot, heat the oil over medium-high heat and sauté the bananas until fragrant and lightly browned. Add the onion, garlic, leek, celery, carrot, and lemongrass. Sauté until the vegetables are soft, about 6 minutes. Add the cumin and cilantro and cook for one minute more until fragrant. Add the orange juice and vegetable stock. Increase the heat and bring the soup to a boil. Reduce heat and simmer for 10 minutes.

Allow the soup to cool enough to handle. Working in batches, carefully puree in a blender. Add the soup back to the pot and stir in the coconut milk. Heat gently and serve in large bowls scattered with cilantro leaves.

Tom Kha Gai
(Thai Chicken Coconut Soup)

1   quart chicken stock

2   cloves garlic, smashed

1   (2-inch) piece fresh ginger, peeled and sliced

2   slices galangal root*

3   kaffir lime leaves**, torn

2   stalks lemongrass, white part only, sliced in half lengthwise

1   teaspoon sugar

2   boneless, skinless chicken breasts

2   (13-ounce) cans coconut milk

1   to 2 teaspoons sambal oelek (Asian hot chili paste), or to taste

1 1/2   tablespoons fish sauce (nam pla or nuoc mam)

1/2   teaspoon turmeric

1   medium carrot, peeled and shredded

8   ounces button mushrooms, cleaned with a damp cloth and halved

Freshly squeezed juice of 2 limes

4   scallions, thinly sliced

Fresh cilantro, chopped, for garnish

I don't know if this soup is authentically Thai, but I do know that it is exotically wonderful and deceptively easy to make. It definitely borrows from the Thai palate, perfectly infusing the flavors of coconut, chile, and lime. It's the kind of soup you can make mid-week when you're stressed out, hating life, and the weekend seems nowhere in sight.

Place the chicken stock, garlic, ginger, galangal root, lime leaves, lemongrass, and sugar in a large stockpot or Dutch oven and bring to a boil. Add the chicken breasts, reduce heat, and simmer gently until the chicken is just cooked through, about 12 minutes.

Fish the chicken out of the pot and allow it to cool a bit on a cutting board. Meanwhile, remove the galangal root, lemongrass, garlic, ginger, and lime leaves from the broth. Stir in the coconut milk, sambal, fish sauce, turmeric, carrot, mushrooms, and lime juice.

When the chicken is cool enough to handle, cut it into rough chunks or shred it with your fingers and add it back to the pot. Heat the soup through gently to soften the carrots but don't bring back to a boil. Add the scallions, ladle into individual bowls, and garnish with chopped cilantro.

*Galangal root can be found in Asian markets in most cities. If you can't find it, feel free to omit it from the recipe.

**Kaffir lime leaves can also be found in Asian markets. If you can't find them, substitute the grated zest of 1 lime instead.

Classic Manhattan Clam Chowder

Is life in Manhattan leaner and meaner than in New England? If so, it's no wonder that no-nonsense Manhattan clam chowder fits right in.

makes 2 quarts

2 tablespoons unsalted butter

1 cup chopped onion

1 cup chopped celery

1/2 cup diced green pepper

2 (10-ounce) cans clams in their juice

4 (8-ounce) bottles clam juice

1 bay leaf

1/2 teaspoon chopped fresh thyme

1/2 teaspoon chopped fresh oregano

Kosher salt and freshly cracked black pepper, to taste

1/2 cup tomato paste

1 cup diced tomatoes

1 tablespoon cornstarch

1 tablespoon cold water

1/4 cup chopped fresh flat-leaf parsley, for garnish

In a large stockpot or Dutch oven over medium heat, melt the butter and sauté the onions, celery, and green pepper until tender, about 5 minutes. Drain the liquid from the canned clams and combine with enough bottled clam juice to make 4 cups.

Add the clams, clam juice, bay leaf, thyme, and oregano and season with salt and pepper. Cover and simmer, 1 hour.

Stir in the tomato paste and tomatoes. Simmer 5 minutes. Meanwhile, mix the cornstarch with the cold water and pour into the simmering soup; stir until slightly thickened. Ladle into large bowls and shower with chopped parsley.

French Mushroom Soup

This soup is all you need for a perfect start to any meal, or as a satisfyingly light meal in its own right. I use cremini mushrooms (baby portobellos) because I like their color and flavor, but feel free to use whatever type of mushrooms you like or happen to have on hand.

4	tablespoons (1/2 stick) unsalted butter
1	pound cremini mushrooms, cleaned with a damp cloth and sliced
1/2	cup chopped onion
	Kosher salt and freshly cracked black pepper, to taste
1/2	cup good, dry sherry
2	quarts beef stock
2	cups sliced carrots
	Fresh flat-leaf parsley, chopped, for garnish

In a Dutch oven or a large, heavy-bottom stockpot, melt the butter over medium-high heat and sauté the mushrooms and onions until the onions are translucent and the mushrooms begin to throw off their juices, about 10 minutes. Season with salt and pepper. Add the sherry and cook off the alcohol, about 1 minute. Add the beef stock and carrots; cover and simmer until the carrots are tender, about 20 minutes. Adjust seasonings, if needed. Ladle into bowls and garnish the soup with chopped parsley.

The Main Attraction

When you have neither the time nor the wherewithal to secure a reservation at the best restaurant in town, you have two choices: You can, of course, call for take-out, or get in the kitchen and cook dinner yourself. That's not such a far-fetched idea, you know. And if indeed you choose the latter, you're still faced with the eternal question: What should we have for dinner? Look no further than the tempting recipes in this chapter.

Moroccan-Inspired Chicken Tagine

serves 8

2   tablespoons extra-virgin olive oil

6   boneless, skinless chicken breasts, cut into 1-inch strips

Kosher salt and freshly cracked black pepper

1   large onion, sliced into thin rings

2   teaspoons peeled and grated fresh ginger

3   cloves garlic, chopped

1 1/2   tablespoons sweet Hungarian paprika

1/2   teaspoon ground cumin

1/2   teaspoon ground turmeric

1/2   teaspoon ground coriander

1/4   teaspoon ground cinnamon

1/2   teaspoon red pepper flakes

1   (14-ounce) can diced tomatoes in their juice

1/2   cup chicken stock

1/2   cup scallions, chopped

Chicken Tagine is a slow-cooked Moroccan dish whose name refers to the conical pot it cooks in, as well as the savory stew inside. I cook my version in a Dutch oven on the stovetop, for the simple reason that I don't own a tagine. Yet, the flavors and the spirit of a real tagine are all here in this simplified recipe, which cooks in about a quarter of the time of the traditional version.

Heat the oil in a Dutch oven or a large, heavy-bottom stockpot over medium-high heat until almost smoking. Season the chicken with salt and pepper and sear in 2 batches until golden brown on all sides, about 6 minutes. Remove the chicken and set aside. Add the onion and ginger to the pan and sauté in the pan drippings over low heat until the onions are translucent, 7 to 10 minutes. Feel free to add another splash of oil if the pan is too dry. Add the garlic, paprika, cumin, turmeric, coriander, cinnamon, and red pepper flakes and sauté until fragrant, 1 minute. Add the tomatoes and chicken stock and bring to a boil. Return the chicken to the pan along with any accumulated juices. Reduce heat, cover, and simmer gently, 15 minutes. Stir in the scallions and serve over Apricot Couscous (page 122).

Cheese Ravioli with Pumpkin Sauce

serves 4

Cheese Ravioli with Pumpkin Sauce is one of my favorites for a quick lunch or dinner. I had something similar at a restaurant in L.A. and I was so smitten, I came home and re-created it from memory.

1   tablespoon extra-virgin olive oil

1/3   cup thinly sliced scallions

2   cloves garlic, minced

1/2   teaspoon fennel seeds

1   cup evaporated skim milk

1   tablespoon all-purpose flour

     Kosher salt and freshly cracked black pepper, to taste

1/2   cup canned pumpkin puree

2   (9-ounce) packages fresh cheese ravioli

     Freshly grated Parmesan, for garnish

Put a large pot of water over high heat to boil. Place the oil, scallions, garlic, and fennel seeds in a medium sauté pan over medium heat. Sauté until the scallions are tender and the fennel seeds are fragrant, about 3 minutes.

Meanwhile, in a small bowl, whisk together the evaporated skim milk, flour, salt, and pepper. Pour into the pan, add the pumpkin, and stir until smooth. Reduce heat and simmer gently while preparing the ravioli.

Generously salt the boiling water and cook the ravioli according to package directions. Fresh pasta cooks in about 2 minutes, so whatever you do, don't abandon it. Drain the pasta and place in a serving dish. Generously spoon the sauce over it. Embellish with plenty of grated Parmesan.

Sweet and Spicy Glazed Salmon Filets

serves 4

Nonstick cooking spray

3 tablespoons dark brown sugar

1 tablespoon low-sodium soy sauce

4 teaspoons Chinese-style mustard

1 teaspoon unseasoned rice vinegar

4 (6-ounce) salmon filets

Kosher salt and freshly cracked black pepper

These salmon filets are shellacked with a sweet, salty, and sticky glaze that's balanced with just the right amount of spicy heat. Mango and Black Bean Salsa (page 130) is the perfect accompaniment.

Preheat the oven to 425°F.

Line a sheet pan with parchment paper and spray it with nonstick cooking spray.

In a small saucepan over medium heat combine the brown sugar, soy sauce, mustard, and rice vinegar and bring just to a boil. Remove from heat.

Meanwhile, place the salmon on the prepared pan and season with salt and pepper. Bake for 12 to 15 minutes, to desired doneness. Remove from oven.

Preheat the broiler.

Brush the glaze evenly over the salmon and broil 3 inches from the heat for 1 to 2 minutes to caramelize the glaze. Serve immediately.

John's Coffee Steak

FOR THE COFFEE RUB

1/2 cup coarsely ground coffee beans

1/4 cup kosher salt

1/4 cup coarsely ground black pepper

1/4 cup packed dark brown sugar

FOR THE STEAKS

2 tablespoons canola oil

4 (8-ounce) New York or rib eye steaks

I first heard the idea of coating a big juicy piece of steak with coffee grounds from my friend John. It seemed strange, to say the least. Then I read an article about a restaurant in Seattle that featured something similar and it was all the rage. So I gave it a try. My first attempts were entirely too peppery, leaving my lips numb for hours, but I finally got it right. The coffee rub forms a beautiful, almost black crust on the outside, and as you cut into the steak it gives way to the tender pink meat inside. One bite and I was hooked! Take my word, however odd it may sound, it's a killer combination. Thanks, John!

Preheat the oven to 400°F.

To make the dry rub, place the coffee, salt, pepper, and brown sugar in a small bowl and toss gently with a fork to combine.

To make the steaks, heat the canola oil in a large, heavy, ovenproof skillet (preferably cast-iron) over high heat until almost smoking. Pat the steaks dry with paper towels and generously and evenly coat all sides with the coffee rub, pressing it in a bit. Any leftover rub can be stored in the freezer for another time. Sear well to form a good crust, 2 to 3 minutes per side. Don't panic if the steaks look a little charred, that's what you're going for and will ensure lots of flavor. Transfer the skillet to the hot oven and cook 5 to 7 minutes for medium-rare, or until desired doneness. Remove to a platter and let the meat rest for 5 to 10 minutes before devouring.

Herb-Crusted Pork Tenderloin Two Ways (With and Without Dijon)

serves **4**

I love a good two-for-one recipe, and this certainly fits the bill. I've been doing Herb-Crusted Rack of Lamb (page 85) for years, and one day it occurred to me, "Why not try it with pork tenderloin?" It works beautifully, whether you make it with or without Dijon. I often prepare it both ways, and let my guests decide. Just use two tenderloins, roughly a pound each, and halve the measurements for the two herb mixtures.

WITH DIJON

- 1/2 cup finely chopped fresh oregano
- 1/2 cup finely chopped fresh thyme
- 1/2 cup finely chopped fresh sage
- 2 tablespoons minced garlic
- 2 tablespoons good Dijon mustard

WITHOUT DIJON

- 1/2 cup finely chopped fresh oregano
- 1/2 cup finely chopped fresh thyme
- 1/2 cup finely chopped fresh sage
- 2 tablespoons minced garlic
- 4 tablespoons extra-virgin olive oil

FOR THE TENDERLOIN

- 2 pounds pork tenderloin, trimmed

  Kosher salt and freshly cracked black pepper
- 3 tablespoons extra-virgin olive oil

Preheat the oven to 400°F.

For the herb crust, in a small bowl, combine the oregano, thyme, sage, garlic, and Dijon (or oil).

To make the tenderloin, generously season it with salt and pepper and rub with the herb mixture. Heat the oil in a large, ovenproof sauté pan (preferably cast-iron) over high heat until almost smoking. Sear the tenderloin on all sides until brown, about 6 minutes. Transfer to the oven and roast until a meat thermometer registers 155°F, about 15 to 20 minutes. Allow the tenderloin to rest, loosely tented under a piece of foil, for 10 minutes to allow the juices to redistribute. Slice on an angle and serve immediately.

Mushroom Ragu over Soft Polenta

serves 2

If the idea of making polenta seems daunting to you, don't worry. I am by no means suggesting that you stand stove-side for 30 minutes, stirring and stirring a pot of cornmeal into oblivion. I get around that here by using instant polenta, which, in my book, is just as good for a quick supper. This is a satisfying, rustic dish, the kind I imagine eating in front of a roaring fire with a nice glass of red wine.

2	tablespoons extra-virgin olive oil
1/2	medium onion, chopped
1	pound cremini mushrooms, cleaned with a damp cloth and sliced
3	tablespoons chopped fresh oregano
1	teaspoon kosher salt
1/2	teaspoon freshly cracked black pepper
1	(14-ounce) can diced tomatoes with their juice
1 1/2	cups instant polenta
1/2	cup grated Gruyère cheese, for garnish

Heat the oil in a large skillet over medium heat; add the onion and cook until tender, about 5 minutes. Stir in the mushrooms and oregano. Season well with salt and pepper and cook until the mushrooms are tender, about 5 minutes. Stir in the tomatoes and simmer until heated through, another 5 minutes.

Meanwhile, in a large saucepan, cook the polenta according to package directions. To serve, spoon the mushroom ragu over the polenta and top with grated cheese.

Herb-Marinated Shrimp

serves 8

Patience may be a virtue, but not when it comes to my dinner. I tend to favor bold flavors I can get on the table quickly. These shrimp never disappoint.

2   cups chopped fresh herbs, such as basil, parsley, thyme, oregano

4   cloves garlic, chopped

3/4   cup extra-virgin olive oil

     Kosher salt and freshly cracked black pepper

12   jumbo shrimp (about 1 1/2 pounds), peeled and deveined with tails on

Combine the herbs, garlic, and oil in a medium bowl or gallon-size resealable plastic bag. Season with salt and pepper and add shrimp. Stir, or shake the bag, to evenly coat the shrimp. Place in the refrigerator and marinate, 45 minutes to 1 hour.

Preheat an outdoor grill or indoor grill pan over high heat.*

Remove the shrimp from the marinade and shake off the excess oil. Grill the shrimp, turning once, just until they curl in on themselves, turn opaque pink, and are firm to the touch. Serve immediately.

*This recipe can also be done on a sheet pan in a 400°F oven. Depending on the size of the shrimp, 10 to 12 minutes should be about all they need.

Easy Linguine with Clams and Fresh Herbs

serves 2

This is one of those easy, elegant dishes that always impress but couldn't be simpler. The clams look so regal perched on top of the linguine.

Kosher salt and freshly cracked black pepper, to taste

8   ounces linguine

2   tablespoons extra-virgin olive oil

2   cloves garlic, chopped

2   (6-ounce) cans chopped clams with their juice

1   tablespoon chopped fresh basil

1   tablespoon chopped fresh tarragon

1   tablespoon chopped fresh flat-leaf parsley

18 small fresh clams (Manila or tiny littleneck), scrubbed*

1/4 cup heavy cream

Put a large pot of water on to boil. Generously salt the water after it comes to a boil and add the linguine; cook according to package directions. Drain.

Meanwhile, in a large sauté pan over medium-high heat, heat the oil. Add the garlic and sauté until fragrant, about 30 seconds. Add the canned clams and their juice, along with the basil, tarragon, parsley, and fresh clams. Cover, reduce the heat to medium, and cook just until the clams open up, 5 to 6 minutes. Transfer the fresh clams to a plate, discarding any that have not opened. Add the cream to the pan, stirring to combine, and season with salt and pepper. Add the cooked linguine and toss with the sauce until all of the pasta is coated. Serve the pasta in big bowls with the fresh clams on top.

Fresh clams should be tightly closed (so that you can't pull them apart), or should close tightly when the shell is tapped. Don't buy clams with open or cracked shells. Discard any clams that haven't opened after steaming.

Pistachio-Crusted Salmon Filets serves 4

4 (6-ounce) boneless, skinless salmon filets

1 cup storebought basil pesto

1½ cups unsalted pistachios, shelled, chopped

I know what you're thinking: Any recipe with the word "crusted" in the title automatically sounds intimidating, complicated, and "chefy." Relax! Pistachio-Crusted Salmon Filets are among my favorite things to make for dinner parties. Not only do they have great stage presence, they are ridiculously easy to prepare. I promise you, if you can chop nuts, you can make this dish. Just make sure not to pulverize the pistachios; it's important to walk that fine line between chopped nuts and pistachio dust.

Preheat the oven to 375°F.

Line a sheet pan with parchment paper. Place the salmon filets on the sheet pan and spread the pesto sauce over the tops and sides. Press the chopped pistachios into the salmon to form a crust. Be generous with the pistachios; you want to form a good crust.

Bake for 10 to 12 minutes, depending on the size of the filets. My idea of the perfect salmon filet is slightly undercooked so you can still see that coral pink trail running through the middle of the fish.

Salt Steak serves 6

This is my idea of red meat perfection, a big juicy steak, all beautifully seared and crusty on the outside, yet tender and pink on the inside. This method of grilling the meat, on a bed of coarse salt (1 1/2 cups!), doesn't make the meat taste too salty, as you might think. Instead, it keeps the meat incredibly tender and seasons it perfectly. This idea is loosely based on a cooking technique used in Italy and France for cooking chicken and whole fish. If you've never dealt with London broil before, it's important to remember a couple of things: For really tender meat, it needs to be cooked to medium-rare, sliced thin on an angle, and always, always cut across the grain.

2	to 2 1/2 pounds London broil
1 1/2	cups kosher salt
	Freshly cracked black pepper
2 1/2	sticks unsalted butter
3	cloves garlic, minced
1/4	cup chopped fresh flat-leaf parsley
1	loaf sliced French bread (sandwich-style)

Preheat an outdoor grill to high heat.

On a plate, layer 3 plain white paper towels one on top of the other and place the meat on top of the paper towels. Allow the meat to sit for several minutes so the juices soak the towels, leaving behind an impression of the meat. Remove the meat and fill the impression with an even layer of salt, about 1/2 inch thick. Season the meat generously with pepper on both sides and place it on the salt.

Lay the whole thing on the grill. (Don't be alarmed when the dry edges of the paper towel catch fire and burn up almost immediately; the soaked portion of towel will be fine.) Grill the meat for about 10 to 12 minutes per side, turning it once back onto the paper towel. For medium-rare, it's done when an instant-read thermometer registers 130° to 140°F. Transfer the meat to a cutting board and allow it to rest for 10 minutes.

Meanwhile, in a medium saucepan over low heat, melt the butter with the garlic and allow the flavors to infuse for a few minutes. Pour the butter into a shallow pie dish and stir in the chopped parsley.

To serve, slice the London broil diagonally across the grain into thin strips. Quickly dip one side of each piece of bread into the melted garlic butter and place butter side up on a plate. Lay several slices of meat over the bread and dig in greedily.

Herb-Crusted Rack of Lamb with Port Demi-Glace

serves 4

Rack of lamb is one of the great culinary cons, a dish that conjures up images of fancy restaurant fare you couldn't possibly re-create in your own kitchen. The truth is, it's one of the easiest and most impressive dishes you can make. You buy the racks already frenched (I'll get to that in a minute)*. You chop some fresh herbs. You mix them with a little Dijon mustard. You pan-sear the racks quickly for a little color. You toss the whole thing in the oven for a few minutes. Voila! A fancy gourmet dinner in no time.

FOR THE LAMB

1/4 cup good Dijon mustard

1/2 cup finely chopped fresh basil

1/2 cup finely chopped fresh thyme

1/2 cup finely chopped fresh oregano

Kosher salt and freshly cracked black pepper, to taste

2 (8-bone) lamb racks, frenched

4 tablespoons extra-virgin olive oil

FOR THE DEMI-GLACE

1 cup good port wine

2 cups veal or beef stock

1 sprig fresh thyme

Kosher salt and freshly cracked black pepper, to taste

Preheat the oven to 450°F.

To prepare the lamb, in a small bowl, combine the mustard, basil, thyme, and oregano; season with salt and pepper. Rub the lamb racks with 2 tablespoons oil, then the herb and mustard mixture to coat. Allow to stand at room temperature 1 hour.

In a large, ovenproof sauté pan or cast-iron skillet, heat the remaining 2 tablespoons oil over high heat until almost smoking. Sear the meat, placing fat side down first, until brown, about 5 minutes per side. Transfer the sauté pan to the oven and roast until a meat thermometer registers 125°F for rare and 130°F for medium-rare, about 15 minutes.

Meanwhile, to make the demi-glace, pour the port wine into a medium saucepan set over medium-high heat and reduce to 1 tablespoon liquid. Add the stock and the thyme sprig and reduce liquid by two thirds. It will be slightly thick and syrupy. Season with pepper, but taste before adding any salt because canned stocks and broths tend to be a bit salty.

Remove lamb racks from oven, and allow them to rest for about 10 minutes, loosely tented under aluminum foil. To serve, cut the racks into individual ribs and serve with Perfect Mashed Potatoes (page 126) and drizzled with demi-glace.

*The term frenching means to clean the meat or fat along the bones on the rib ends. It makes for a fancy presentation. If you can't find racks already frenched, ask your butcher to do it for you.

Seafood Scampi serves 6

This recipe is an homage to a wonderful seafood dish I had for lunch in Laguna Beach, recently. It was so good I went back that same evening and had it again for dinner! The butter sauce was delicately flecked with parsley, garlic, and, surprisingly, basil. And the simple addition of fresh tomatoes really brightened things up. This dish is best served over white rice or with big hunks of crusty Italian bread to sop up the juice.

1/2	cup chopped fresh flat-leaf parsley
8	tablespoons (1 stick) unsalted butter, room temperature
1/4	cup fresh lemon juice
2	tablespoons heavy cream
1	teaspoon Worcestershire sauce
4	cloves garlic, minced
1	pound sea scallops
1	pound medium shrimp, shelled and deveined
	Kosher salt and freshly cracked black pepper
4	tablespoons extra-virgin olive oil
1/4	cup good, dry white wine
2	plum tomatoes, seeded and chopped
1/2	bunch fresh basil leaves
	Lemon wedges, for garnish
	Crusty French bread, for dipping

In a small bowl, combine the parsley, butter, lemon juice, cream, Worcestershire sauce, and garlic, mashing together with a fork.

Pat the seafood dry with a paper towel and season generously with salt and pepper. In a large sauté pan, heat 2 tablespoons oil over medium-high heat until almost smoking. Sear the scallops until they caramelize and turn opaque, 1 1/2 to 2 minutes per side. Resist the urge to touch or poke at the scallops so that caramelization has the chance to occur. Transfer to a plate and tent loosely with foil to keep warm.

Meanwhile, heat the remaining 2 tablespoons oil in the same pan. Sauté the shrimp just until pink and curled, 2 to 3 minutes. Remove the shrimp to the same plate as the scallops. Add the wine to the pan, stirring up the browned bits, then add the tomatoes; cook until the pan is almost dry.

Meanwhile, make a chiffonade of the basil: Stack the leaves, roll them into a cigar shape, and thinly slice into fine ribbons. Add the basil to the pan and stir in the butter mixture until just melted. Remove from heat and stir in the seafood. Garnish with lemon wedges and serve immediately, with crusty bread on the side.

Fresh Cheese Ravioli
with Sage Brown Butter serves 4

Kosher salt and freshly cracked black pepper, to taste

2 (9-ounce) packages fresh cheese ravioli

1 tablespoon extra-virgin olive oil

12 whole fresh sage leaves, plus 2 tablespoons coarsely chopped

6 tablespoons unsalted butter

1/2 teaspoon chopped fresh thyme

2 tablespoons chopped fresh flat-leaf parsley, for garnish

If you live in fear of carbs, look away now. If, however, you are the type who chooses not to give into dietary trends and throws all caution to the wind, keep reading! This is my take on the classic recipe of nutty browned butter and soft pillows of cheesy ravioli with fresh sage leaves. The unapologetic use of store-bought refrigerator ravioli makes this a quick meal for busy weeknights or whenever the craving strikes.

Put a large pot of water over high heat to boil. When it comes to a boil, generously salt the water and cook the ravioli according to the package directions; do not overcook.

Meanwhile, in a medium sauté pan, heat the oil over high heat. Add the whole sage leaves and fry about 1 minute on each side until lightly crisp. Remove to a paper towel to drain.

In the same sauté pan, melt the butter over medium-high heat, allowing it to brown slightly to develop its nutty flavor. Stir in the chopped sage and thyme. Season with salt and pepper.

Drain the pasta and place on a serving platter. Generously spoon the sage butter sauce over the ravioli and shower with the fried sage leaves and a generous sprinkling of chopped parsley. Serve immediately.

Chicken Crêpes

FOR THE CRÊPES

1   cup all-purpose flour

1/4   teaspoon kosher salt

3   large eggs

2   tablespoons unsalted butter, melted, plus more for the pan

1   cup milk, plus more if needed

FOR THE FILLING

2   tablespoons extra-virgin olive oil

1¹/3   pound diced chicken tenders

1   medium onion, diced

1/2   pound cremini mushrooms, cleaned with a damp cloth and sliced

1   (8-ounce) brick cream cheese, room temperature

2   tablespoons chopped fresh sage leaves

    Kosher salt and freshly cracked black pepper, to taste

FOR THE GRAVY

2   tablespoons unsalted butter

1   shallot, chopped

4   cremini mushrooms, cleaned with a damp cloth and finely chopped

2   tablespoons all-purpose flour

1   cup chicken stock

    Kosher salt and freshly cracked black pepper, to taste

    Fresh flat-leaf parsley, chopped, for garnish

To make the crêpes, in the bowl of a freestanding mixer fitted with a whisk attachment, mix the flour, salt, and eggs until smooth; add the melted butter and mix thoroughly. Slowly add the milk and whisk until the batter is the consistency of heavy cream. If it's too thick, add more milk, 1 tablespoon at a time, until it's the right consistency. Cover and refrigerate the batter for at least 1 hour.

Meanwhile, to make the filling, place the oil in a medium sauté pan over medium-high heat and add the chicken; cook until brown, about 3 minutes. Add the onions and mushrooms and sauté until onions are translucent and mushrooms are tender, 6 to 8 minutes. Set aside to cool slightly. Tip the chicken mixture into a medium bowl; mix in the cream cheese and chopped sage. Season with salt and pepper.

Heat a 7-inch, nonstick skillet over medium-high heat; brush with melted butter. Pour about 3 tablespoons crêpe batter into the pan and swirl to coat the bottom evenly. Cook until the top of the crêpe appears dry, loosening the sides with a heat-resistant rubber spatula, about 45 seconds. Flip the crêpe over and cook until brown spots appear on the second side, about 30 seconds. Turn the crêpe out onto a plate. Repeat with remaining batter, stacking crêpes on top of one another.

There is something so satisfying about pairing a bit of elegance with the everyday. Here, Southern food plays dress-up, with delicate crêpes surrounding a hearty, savory filling.

Preheat the oven to 350°F.

To assemble the crêpes, place about 3 tablespoons filling in a line down the center of each crêpe. Fold over in thirds and place seam side down in a baking dish. Cover with foil and heat crêpes through, 12 to 15 minutes.

While the crêpes are warming, get on with the gravy. Heat the butter over medium-high heat in a medium sauté pan, add the shallots and the mushrooms, and cook until the shallots are tender, about 3 minutes. Stir in the flour; cook 1 minute. Whisk in the chicken stock and bring to a boil. Reduce the gravy for about 1 minute until thick and creamy, season with salt and pepper. Drizzle the gravy artfully over the crêpes and sprinkle with chopped parsley for color. Serve immediately.

Spaghetti alla Carbonara

serves 6

Spaghetti alla Carbonara was big in the '70s, but like so many food trends of that decade, it fell out of fashion for a while. I think it's time to reissue this simple classic. By simple I mean its preparation, not its flavor. There are several theories on the origin of Spaghetti alla Carbonara, which means, "spaghetti in the manner of coal miners." It's rumored that the Italians created the dish during World War II when American servicemen were hungry for bacon and eggs. My favorite legend however, claims that it was a staple of the coal miner diet because its few and simple ingredients could easily be carried into the mines and they needed no refrigeration. A roaring campfire was all that was required for a quick meal. The liberal use of black pepper in the dish is said to represent the flecks of coal that would fall onto the miner's plates.

Kosher salt and freshly cracked black pepper

1 1/4 pounds spaghetti

4 cloves garlic

3 tablespoons extra-virgin olive oil

1/2 pound thickly sliced pancetta, cut into 1/4-inch cubes

1/4 cup good, dry white wine

2 large eggs*

1/3 cup freshly grated Pecorino Romano cheese

1/4 cup freshly grated Parmigiano-Reggiano cheese

3 tablespoons chopped fresh flat-leaf parsley

*If you're concerned about using raw eggs, substitute 1/2 cup pasteurized egg product for 2 large eggs.

Bring a large pot of water to a boil; generously season the water with salt. Cook the spaghetti according to package directions, to al dente. Reserve 1/4 cup of the pasta cooking water.

Meanwhile, with the flat side of a butcher knife, smash the garlic cloves and place them in a medium sauté pan along with the oil over medium-high heat. Sauté until the garlic turns golden, about 2 minutes. Remove the garlic and discard. Place the pancetta in the pan and cook until it begins to crisp around the edges, about 5 minutes. Add the wine and let the alcohol cook off, about 1 minute. Remove from the heat.

Crack the eggs into a large serving bowl and beat them lightly with a fork. Add the reserved pasta water and whisk to temper the eggs. Add the cheeses and a generous grinding of black pepper, along with the parsley. Mix well.

Drain the spaghetti and immediately add to the bowl. Tip the pancetta into the bowl and toss well to coat. Serve immediately.

Salmon with Leeks in Parchment Paper

serves 4

I'm convinced that one reason we Americans are so put off by the idea of cooking French food is that it sounds so fussy and complicated. Without a doubt, some of it is. But allow me to enter this dish into evidence. The French refer to it as Saumon en Papillote. Loosely translated, it means "salmon in paper." Inside the paper packet, the fish steams gently and mingles with the wine, leeks, and lemon, creating its own delicate sauce. If that's not enough to tempt you, ask yourself, when else in your adult life do you have a legitimate excuse to cut out paper hearts?

4   sheets parchment paper (about 14 inches)

4   (6- to 8-ounce) boneless, skinless salmon filets

      Kosher salt and freshly cracked black pepper

1   large leek, white part only, cleaned and thinly sliced*

4   tablespoons (1/2 stick) unsalted butter, melted

1/2   cup good, dry white wine

4   sprigs fresh dill

8   paper-thin slices lemon

Preheat the oven to 400°F.

Fold each sheet of parchment paper in half and cut into the fold, creating a half-heart shape about 4 inches bigger than the salmon. Open the parchment hearts and lay one flat on a work surface. Season one of the salmon filets with salt and pepper and center on the parchment paper heart close to the fold. Lay a small handful of leeks (about 1/4 cup) alongside the salmon next to the fold and drizzle the whole thing with 1 tablespoon melted butter and 2 tablespoons wine. Gently tear the leaves off of a sprig of dill and scatter them over the salmon and leeks. Top the filet with two overlapping slices of lemon and fold parchment heart closed over the salmon. Beginning at the curve of the heart, make small overlapping folds to seal the edges of the paper entirely and create an enclosed packet. Tuck the tail end under and make sure there are no gaps in the seal. Repeat with the remaining paper and salmon.

Place the packets on a sheet pan and bake until the edges of the paper are slightly browned and the salmon is firm to the touch, 12 to 15 minutes. To serve, carefully cut open the parchment packets, being careful of the hot steam.

*Leeks grow in loose, sandy soil and must be cleaned properly before using. I generally cut them in half lengthwise, slice them thin, and swish them around a bowl full of cold water. All of the grit will drop to the bottom. Dry thoroughly on paper towels.

Grilled Asian Skirt Steak

serves 4

This recipe plays on my love of cinnamon paired with red meat, though not quite as intensely as with the Cinnamon-Kissed Moroccan Beef Stew (page 108). Here it's more of a subtle background note that mingles nicely with the ginger, garlic, and sherry. I like to marinate this steak as long as possible, but I've also made it when it's only had an hour in the marinade and it was delicious.

FOR THE MARINADE

1   (6-inch) piece of ginger, peeled and sliced

4   cloves garlic, sliced

4   teaspoons dark-brown sugar

1   teaspoon ground cinnamon

6   cinnamon sticks

1/2 cup good, dry sherry

6   tablespoons low-sodium soy sauce

1/4 cup extra-virgin olive oil

FOR THE STEAK

2   small skirt steaks (about 1 pound each)

     Kosher salt and freshly cracked black pepper

     Fresh cilantro leaves, roughly chopped, for garnish

To make the marinade, in a medium bowl, combine the ginger, garlic, brown sugar, ground cinnamon, cinnamon sticks, sherry, and soy sauce. Whisk in the oil and pour the marinade over the steak in a heavy, gallon-size resealable bag. Marinate for at least 30 minutes at room temperature, or for several hours in the refrigerator. The longer the meat swims in the marinade, the more flavorful it will be.

Preheat an outdoor grill over high heat or an indoor grill pan until almost smoking.

Remove the steak from the marinade and brush off any slices of garlic and ginger, as they'll just burn and char on the grill. Place the meat on a bed of several layers of paper towels and blot off as much of the liquid as possible. If the meat is too wet it won't sear, it will steam, which will result in a gray steak. Season both sides generously with salt and pepper.

Grill the steak without moving it around or poking it so it has a chance to sear and get those beautiful grill marks, about 4 minutes per side for medium-rare. For really tender meat, I don't recommend cooking it beyond that. Transfer to a cutting board and allow the meat to rest, loosely tented under aluminum foil, for at least 5 minutes. Slice into thin strips across the grain and scatter with a shower of chopped cilantro.

Shrimp in White Wine and Cream Sauce

serves 4

Shrimp have the distinction of being able to take on whatever flavors you throw at them. While not the most glamorous of all sea creatures, they certainly can be, especially when paired with sophisticated flavors like the ones below. Believe me, but this dish requires very little in the way of effort and has great stage presence.

3	tablespoons unsalted butter
1	shallot, minced
1 1/2	pounds medium or large shrimp, peeled and deveined
1/2	teaspoon chopped fresh thyme
1	bay leaf
	Kosher salt and freshly cracked black pepper
2	tablespoons good brandy
3/4	cup good, dry white wine
1	cup heavy cream
2	egg yolks
1	teaspoon freshly squeezed lemon juice
1	teaspoon chopped fresh flat-leaf parsley, plus more for garnish
1	teaspoon chopped fresh chervil
1	teaspoon chopped fresh tarragon

In a medium sauté pan over medium heat, melt the butter and sauté the shallot until soft, about 3 minutes. Add the shrimp, thyme, bay leaf, salt, and pepper; sauté until the shrimp are opaque, 7 to 8 minutes. Remove from the heat. Add the brandy and carefully light it by tipping the pan toward the flame. If you have an electric stove, light the brandy with a grill lighter. Shake the pan back and forth until the flame dies and the alcohol burns off, about 1 minute. Remove the shrimp with a slotted spoon to a heated serving dish to keep warm. Stir the wine into the sauce and simmer for 5 minutes to cook off the alcohol.

Meanwhile, in a small bowl, combine the cream, egg yolks, lemon juice, parsley, chervil, and tarragon. Add the cream mixture to the pan; stir to heat through, but do not boil. Add the shrimp back to the pan, turn to coat and warm through. Shower the remaining chopped parsley over the whole thing. Beautiful!

Penne with Mushrooms and Asparagus

serves 4

Where is it written that you have to serve Beef Wellington or some other complicated dish at a dinner party? At one of my best parties ever, I served TV dinners. My friends loved it! I'm not suggesting that you serve TV dinners the next time you entertain, but why not keep it simple? This pasta dish is easy, elegant, and takes almost no time to put together.

Kosher salt and freshly cracked black pepper, to taste

4 cups penne pasta

16 asparagus spears, cut into 1-inch pieces

4 tablespoons unsalted butter

4 tablespoons extra-virgin olive oil

8 ounces wild mushrooms, sliced (enoki, chanterelle, cremini, portobello, shiitake, or oyster mushrooms)

4 cloves garlic, minced

4 tablespoons chopped shallots

4 tablespoons good white wine

1/2 cup chicken stock

2 teaspoons chopped fresh flat-leaf parsley

2 teaspoons chopped fresh tarragon

2 teaspoons chopped fresh chervil

2 teaspoons chopped fresh chives

1/2 cup freshly grated Parmesan cheese

White truffle oil, for drizzling

Bring a large pot of water to a boil, then generously season with salt. Cook the penne according to package directions, to al dente. Reserve 1/2 cup of the pasta cooking water.

Meanwhile, blanch the asparagus: Bring a large pot of water to a boil and generously season with salt. Fill a large bowl with ice water and push a colander or mesh strainer down into the water. Plunge the asparagus into boiling water and cook for 45 seconds to 1 minute, depending on the thickness of the spears. The asparagus should be bright green and maintain its "bite." Remove the asparagus and immediately plunge into the ice bath. This will "shock" the asparagus and stop the cooking process. Drain well.

In a large sauté pan, heat the butter and oil over medium-high heat. Add the mushrooms; cook 1 to 2 minutes. Reduce heat; add the garlic and shallots and cook until the shallots are soft, about 2 minutes. Add the wine and cook until evaporated, about 30 seconds. Add the chicken stock and cook until the mushrooms are tender and pan is almost dry. Add the cooked penne and the reserved cooking water along with the herbs, asparagus, and Parmesan cheese. Season with salt and pepper. Cook until just heated through. Turn the pasta out onto plates and drizzle with truffle oil.

Cold-Poached Salmon
with White Nectarine Salsa serves 4

FOR THE SALMON

1   quart chicken or fish stock

    Zest of 2 limes, removed with a vegetable peeler

4   sprigs fresh mint

4   (8-ounce) boneless, skinless salmon filets

FOR THE SALSA

2   ripe white nectarines, halved, pitted, and diced

1   jalapeño pepper, seeded and minced

1/2   red bell pepper, diced

1   tablespoon chopped fresh cilantro

1   tablespoon chopped fresh mint

    Freshly squeezed juice of 1 lime

1   teaspoon sugar (optional, depending on the sweetness of the fruit)

    Kosher salt and freshly cracked black pepper, to taste

I recently read with great fascination about the technique of cold-poaching fish. I was very excited by the notion of pouring hot liquid over a piece of raw fish, and by the time it cools to room temperature, it's completely cooked through with little more effort than heating a bit of stock. Of course, this hardly qualifies as cooking, which eliminates any excuse you may have for not trying this recipe. Paired with White Nectarine Salsa, it's the perfect summer meal.

To prepare the salmon, heat the stock, lime zest, and mint sprigs in a medium saucepan until just under a boil. Place the salmon filets in a glass baking dish deep enough to be covered by the stock. Pour the hot stock over the salmon and let stand 5 minutes. Turn the fish over and let stand for 1 hour until the salmon and stock are both room temperature.

Meanwhile, to make the salsa, in a small bowl combine the nectarines, jalapeño, red bell pepper, cilantro, mint, lime juice, and sugar, if using. Season with salt and pepper.

Remove the fish from the stock and serve with the White Nectarine Salsa over the top.

Thai Marinated Beef

It may seem odd, even surprising, to suggest using fish sauce in a marinade for steak. Trust me, it won't add even the slightest hint of "fishiness" to the meat. Instead, the pungent sauce, while not appetizing on its own, lends a salty, deep flavor to the marinade and is a key ingredient in many Thai recipes.

serves 2

2	tablespoons minced garlic
2	tablespoons minced fresh cilantro
1	tablespoon white peppercorns
1 1/2	tablespoons fish sauce (nam pla or nuoc mam)*
1 1/2	tablespoons low-sodium soy sauce
1	tablespoon sugar
2	(8-ounce) New York strip or rib eye steaks

Combine the garlic, cilantro, white peppercorns, fish sauce, soy sauce, and sugar in a blender and process until smooth. Rub the marinade all over the steaks and allow them to marinate in a gallon-size plastic freezer bag in the refrigerator for at least 1 hour, up to 6 hours if possible. As with most marinades, the longer it sits the better.

Preheat a grill or indoor grill pan over high heat.

Remove the steaks from the marinade and discard marinade. Grill the steaks over a high flame until medium-rare (when a meat thermometer registers 130° to 140°F) or until desired doneness.

Fish sauce can be found in Asian markets in most cities. Some major markets carry it on the Asian aisle.

Sautéed Shrimp

serves 4

with Butter, Garlic, Thyme, and Lemon

This recipe has very few ingredients, packs really big flavor, and requires that you spend very little time in the kitchen. Do you see where I'm going here? So little work, such great reward.

8   tablespoons (1 stick) unsalted butter

4   cloves garlic, minced

4   sprigs fresh thyme, leaves chopped

Grated zest and freshly squeezed juice of 1 lemon

2   pounds jumbo shrimp, peeled and deveined

Kosher salt and freshly cracked black pepper

Fresh flat-leaf parsley, chopped, for garnish

In a large sauté pan over medium-high heat, melt the butter; add the garlic, thyme, and lemon zest, then toss in the shrimp. Turn to coat them in the butter and season with salt and pepper. Sauté the shrimp until they turn coral pink and the tails begin to curl in on themselves. Tumble the shrimp onto a platter, spritz with the lemon juice, and shower with parsley.

Pan-Seared Filet Mignon with Blackberry-Cabernet Sauce

serves 4

There are those who would argue that a good steak needs no adornment, and I tend to agree. But this sauce is sophisticated and unexpected. Give it a try and you'll see what I mean.

FOR THE STEAKS

4 (8-ounce) filet mignon steaks

Kosher salt and freshly cracked black pepper

2 tablespoons extra-virgin olive oil

FOR THE SAUCE

2/3 cup beef stock

2/3 cup Cabernet Sauvignon

3 tablespoons seedless blackberry preserves

Kosher salt and freshly cracked black pepper, to taste

A handful fresh blackberries, for garnish

Preheat the oven to 400°F.

To make the steaks, pat the steaks dry with a paper towel and season generously with salt and pepper. In a heavy, ovenproof skillet, heat the oil over medium-high heat until almost smoking. Sear the steaks, on 1 side only, for 2 to 3 minutes until the meat begins to caramelize. Do not touch or poke at the meat so that caramelization can occur. You want your steaks to have that perfect contrast in texture: seared and crusty on one side, tender and juicy on the other. Without flipping the steak, transfer the pan to the oven and roast for about 7 to 9 minutes for medium-rare (when a meat thermometer registers 130° to 140°F).

Meanwhile, to make the sauce, in a small saucepan combine the beef stock, Cabernet Sauvignon, and blackberry preserves. Bring to a boil. Reduce to a simmer and allow the mixture to reduce by two-thirds. The sauce is ready when it becomes slightly thick and syrupy and coats the back of a spoon. Season with pepper, but taste before adding any salt, because canned stocks tend to be a bit salty.

Remove the steaks from the oven and allow them to rest, loosely tented under a piece of aluminum foil, about 5 minutes. To serve, drizzle the sauce over the steaks and scatter a few blackberries on the plate.

Chicken Breasts
with Basil-Cream Sauce

serves 2

I know, I know! Chicken has been done to death and we're all bored with it. But this chicken recipe is inspired. The flavor combination is classic, the ingredients simple. This is a useful recipe to have up your sleeve for unexpected guests, or a weekday evening when you just can't bear another carton of Chinese take-out.

FOR THE CHICKEN

2　tablespoons extra-virgin olive oil

2　boneless, skinless chicken breasts

　　Kosher salt and freshly cracked black pepper

FOR THE SAUCE

1　cup good, dry white wine

4　egg yolks

1/2　cup heavy cream

1/4　teaspoon kosher salt

　　Freshly cracked black pepper

1　tablespoon freshly squeezed lemon juice

1　tablespoon chopped fresh flat-leaf parsley

2　tablespoons chopped fresh basil

To make the chicken, heat the oil in a medium skillet over medium heat until almost smoking. Meanwhile, season the chicken breasts with salt and pepper. Place the chicken in the pan and cook until the chicken begins to brown, about 3 minutes per side. Remove chicken to a platter and loosely tent with aluminum foil to keep warm. Leave the pan on the burner.

To make the sauce, add the wine to the pan, scraping up the brown bits from the bottom and allow the alcohol to cook off, about 1 minute. In a separate bowl, whisk the yolks, cream, salt, and pepper. Pour the mixture into the pan and cook over low heat, stirring constantly until sauce begins to thicken, about 1 minute. Stir in the lemon juice and return the chicken to the pan. Cover and simmer until the chicken is just cooked through, about 5 minutes. Remove the chicken to a platter and stir the chopped parsley and basil into the sauce. Pour the sauce over the chicken and serve.

Oven-Baked Coconut Shrimp with Pineapple Salsa

serves 4

FOR THE SHRIMP

3   cups shredded sweetened coconut

1   cup all-purpose flour

1/2   cup panko* (Japanese-style bread crumbs)

1   teaspoon cayenne pepper, or to taste

    Kosher salt, to taste

4   large egg whites

1   pound large shrimp, peeled and deveined, tails intact

    Nonstick cooking spray

FOR THE SALSA

1   cup finely diced fresh pineapple

1/3   cup finely minced red onion

1/4   cup finely chopped fresh cilantro

1/4   cup pineapple preserves

1/2   to 1 jalapeño pepper, seeded and minced, to taste

    Freshly squeezed juice of 1 lime

    Kosher salt and freshly cracked black pepper, to taste

*Panko bread crumbs can be found on the Asian aisle of most major grocery stores or in Asian markets.

I experimented with several ways to make coconut shrimp without frying them. Not that I have anything against fried coconut shrimp. I love fried coconut shrimp. I just hate standing over a vat of hot oil, dipping and dredging and frying them up. The key to baking them is to toast the coconut first. It's a subtle thing that makes all the difference.

Preheat the oven to 350°F.

Spread the coconut evenly on an ungreased sheet pan and toast in the oven, stirring occasionally, until golden, 8 to 10 minutes.

Increase oven temperature to 400°F.

To prepare the shrimp, line a sheet pan with parchment paper. In a shallow dish, whisk together the flour, bread crumbs, cayenne pepper, and salt. Place the toasted coconut in another dish. Place the egg whites in a medium bowl and whisk until frothy. Pat the shrimp dry and dip first in the egg whites, then the flour, back in the egg whites, then roll in the coconut. Arrange the shrimp on the prepared pan and spray lightly with cooking spray. Bake 12 to 15 minutes, until cooked through and golden.

To make the salsa, in a small bowl combine the pineapple, red onion, cilantro, pineapple preserves, jalapeño, and lime juice. Season with salt and pepper. Serve alongside the coconut shrimp.

Pan-Roasted New York Strip Steak with Arugula, Roasted Red Peppers, and Balsamic Vinaigrette serves 4

Every chef has a version of this salad. The sweet tanginess of the balsamic vinaigrette is the perfect complement to the savory steak, sweet roasted peppers, and peppery sharp arugula. If in an ambitious mood, you could roast your own peppers, but it's even easier to buy them in a jar. That means dinner on the table in less time. Everybody's happy!

FOR THE STEAKS

- 2 (8-ounce) New York strip steaks, about 1 1/2 inches thick
- Kosher salt and freshly cracked black pepper
- 2 tablespoons extra-virgin olive oil

FOR THE VINAIGRETTE

- 3 tablespoons balsamic vinegar
- 1/4 cup extra-virgin olive oil
- 1/4 teaspoon kosher salt
- 1/4 teaspoon freshly cracked black pepper

FOR THE SALAD

- 2 bags baby arugula
- 1 1/2 cups drained roasted red peppers (2 large peppers)
- 1/2 cup Gorgonzola cheese

To make the steaks, preheat the oven to 400°F.

Pat the steaks dry with a paper towel and season generously with salt and pepper. In a heavy, ovenproof skillet over high heat, heat the oil until almost smoking. Sear the steaks until the meat begins to caramelize, 2 to 3 minutes per side. Do not touch or poke at the meat so that caramelization can occur. Transfer the pan to the oven and roast for about 10 minutes for medium-rare (when a meat thermometer registers 130° to 140°F).

To make the vinaigrette, in a small bowl whisk together the vinegar, olive oil, salt, and pepper. Set aside.

Remove the steaks to a plate and allow them to rest, loosely tented under a piece of aluminum foil, for 5 to 10 minutes.

To make the salads, make a bed of arugula on each plate, slice the peppers into thin strips and arrange over the arugula. Cut the steaks on an angle into 1/4-inch strips and place on top of the salad. Whisk any of the meat juices that have collected on the plate into the dressing and drizzle dressing over the salads. Crumble the Gorgonzola cheese over the top and serve.

Sea Scallops with Gruyère Sauce serves 6

2 pounds large sea scallops

2 tablespoons extra-virgin olive oil

4 tablespoons (1/2 stick) unsalted butter

1/2 pound cremini mushrooms, cleaned with a damp cloth and sliced

1/4 cup minced onion

1/3 cup all-purpose flour

1/2 cup good, dry white wine

1 cup heavy cream

1/2 cup whole milk

Kosher salt and white pepper, to taste

1 cup grated Gruyère cheese

1 tablespoon plus 1 teaspoon freshly squeezed lemon juice

1 tablespoon chopped fresh flat-leaf parsley, for garnish

This is about as close as I get to haute cuisine, mostly because I don't much care for things towered on a plate with dribbles and dabs of fancy sauce, making it look much better than it actually tastes. It's also unrealistic to expect people to cook that way at home. This dish combines elegance and sophistication with simple everyday preparation. Does it get any better than that?

Wash the scallops and pat dry with a paper towel to ensure caramelization when seared. In a large skillet, heat the oil over medium-high heat to almost smoking, and sear the scallops until a golden crust forms, about 2 minutes on each side. Remove to a plate and keep warm under a loosely tented piece of foil.

Add the butter to the pan and sauté the mushrooms and onions for about 5 minutes; add the flour and cook, stirring, 1 minute. Whisk in the wine; cook off the alcohol, about 1 minute. Whisk in the cream and the milk; simmer gently until the sauce begins to thicken, about 2 minutes. Season with salt and white pepper. Add the cheese, stirring until melted. Add the lemon juice. Add the scallops back into the pan; turn the scallops in the sauce to warm through. Serve immediately, garnished with the chopped parsley.

Baja-Style Fried Fish Tacos

serves 4

Okay, admittedly I've never been to Baja. But taco stands that serve Baja-style fish tacos are a staple in Southern California. I swear you can almost imagine yourself standing on the beach in San Felipe when you eat these. Served with an icy cold Mexican beer, there is nothing better.

FOR THE CHIPOTLE SAUCE

1/2 cup mayonnaise

2 tablespoons milk

2 tablespoons freshly squeezed lime juice

1/4 teaspoon chipotle powder, or to taste

FOR THE PICO DE GALLO

3 ripe plum tomatoes, seeded, finely chopped

1/4 cup finely chopped white onion

3 tablespoons chopped fresh cilantro leaves

1 jalapeño pepper, seeded, finely chopped

Freshly squeezed juice of 2 limes

Kosher salt and freshly cracked black pepper, to taste

FOR THE FISH

1 cup all-purpose flour

1 teaspoon kosher salt

1 teaspoon cayenne pepper, or to taste

1 cup pale beer

1 pound boned, skinned white fish (cod, catfish, halibut)

Vegetable oil, for frying

16 soft corn tortillas

1/2 head cabbage, shredded

1 lime, cut into wedges

To make the chipotle sauce, in a medium bowl, combine the mayonnaise, milk, lime juice, and chipotle powder.

To make the pico de gallo, in a medium bowl, combine the tomatoes, onion, cilantro, jalapeño, lime juice, salt, and pepper.

To prepare the fish, in a bowl, whisk together the flour, salt, and cayenne pepper. Whisk in the beer, blending well and making sure there are no lumps; it should be the consistency of thick pancake batter. Rinse the fish and pat dry. Cut into 2-inch pieces.

Pour 1 inch vegetable oil into a large, heavy-bottom frying pan or Dutch oven; heat over high heat until the oil measures 375°F on a deep-fry thermometer. Dip the fish pieces in the beer batter and lift out, draining briefly. Gently slide the coated fish into the hot oil, a few pieces at a time. Adjust the heat to maintain oil temperature. Fry until golden brown, about 2 minutes. Remove fish to a paper towel–lined platter using a slotted spoon or Chinese strainer. Continue with the remaining fish pieces.

Warm the corn tortillas in a preheated 250°F oven or in the microwave. To assemble the tacos, stack two tortillas in your hand. Add a few pieces of fish, some chipotle sauce and pico de gallo, and top with shredded cabbage. Spritz with a squeeze of lime, fold in half, and enjoy!

Cinnamon-Kissed Moroccan Beef Stew

serves 4

1/4 cup vegetable oil, plus more as needed

1 pound beef stew meat, cut into 1-inch cubes

1 cup plus 3 tablespoons all-purpose flour

1 tablespoon freshly cracked black pepper, plus more to taste

2 tablespoons plus 2 teaspoons ground cinnamon

4 cloves garlic, chopped

1 cup good, dry red wine

2 tablespoons balsamic vinegar

2 bay leaves

5 whole cloves

3 cups beef stock

1 large onion, sliced into thin rings

2 large carrots, peeled and cut into chunks

2 small red potatoes, peeled and cut into chunks

Kosher salt, to taste

1/4 cup chopped fresh flat-leaf parsley, for garnish

In a Dutch oven or a large, heavy-bottom, ovenproof stockpot, heat the oil over high heat until almost smoking. Meanwhile, place the beef in a large gallon-size resealable bag along with 1 cup flour. Coat the beef thoroughly and shake off the excess flour (place it in a wire sieve and shake vigorously). Sprinkle the beef liberally with the black pepper and 2 table-spoons cinnamon. Fry the meat in small batches so as not to overcrowd the pan. It's important that the beef sears and gets deep golden brown. Remove the seared beef to a paper towel to drain. Add more oil to the pan if it gets too dry.

Preheat the oven to 350°F.

When you've finished browning all the meat, reduce the heat to medium and add the garlic. Sauté until fragrant, about 30 seconds. Make a roux: Add the remaining 3 tablespoons flour and remaining 2 teaspoons cinnamon and stir constantly for another 1 or 2 minutes, scraping up the brown bits on the bottom of the pan. Whisk in the wine and the balsamic vinegar, again scraping up the browned bits from the bottom of the pan. Toss in the bay leaves and cloves. Bring to a bubble, whisking constantly. Whisk in the beef stock and add the onions, carrots, and potatoes. Season with salt and pepper. Add the beef back into the pan and stir to coat. Cover and place in the oven to cook until the beef is tender, 2 hours. Shower with chopped parsley just before serving.

This is exactly the kind of food I want to eat when it's cold and gray outside. The idea of using cinnamon in a savory dish takes its cues from the Moroccan palate, one I've become quite fond of experimenting with. Try this delicious Moroccan-inspired stew served over Apricot Couscous (page 122).

Chili-Rubbed Flank Steak serves 4

Here's another one for all you steak lovers. Smoky chipotle and chili make for a gutsy rub. Try it and you'll see what I mean.

4   tablespoons chili powder

2   tablespoons ground cumin

2   teaspoons ground chipotle powder

2   teaspoons dried oregano

2   teaspoons dried parsley

2   teaspoons kosher salt

2   pounds flank steak

3   tablespoons extra-virgin olive oil

Preheat the oven to 400°F.

In a small bowl, combine the chili powder, cumin, chipotle, oregano, parsley, and salt. Rub the spice mixture over the steak to coat completely.

In a large, heavy, ovenproof skillet, heat the oil until almost smoking. Sear the steaks until the meat begins to caramelize, 2 to 3 minutes per side; don't touch or poke at the meat so that caramelization can occur. Transfer the pan to the oven and roast for 5 to 6 minutes for medium-rare (when a meat thermometer registers 130° to 140°F).

Remove the steaks to a plate and allow them to rest, loosely tented under a piece of aluminum foil, 5 to 10 minutes. Slice thin across the grain and dig in.

Mango Chicken Salad

serves 4

1/2   cup sweetened, shredded coconut

3/4   cup mayonnaise

1/2   cup chopped fresh cilantro

      Freshly squeezed juice of 1 lime

2   tablespoons Major Grey's mango chutney

1   tablespoon good Dijon mustard

1   teaspoon ground turmeric

1/2   teaspoon cayenne pepper, or to taste

      Kosher salt and freshly cracked black pepper, to taste

4   boneless, skinless chicken breasts, cooked and shredded

1   mango, peeled, seeded and diced

This recipe is the perfect use for leftover grilled or poached chicken. It's made here in the traditional way, with mayonnaise. But if you are struggling to stay on the dietary straight and narrow, feel free to substitute plain yogurt. Your waistline will thank you and the flavor payoff is nearly the same.

Preheat the oven to 350°F.

Spread the coconut evenly on an ungreased sheet pan and toast in the oven, stirring occasionally, until golden, 8 to 10 minutes.

In a medium bowl, whisk together the mayonnaise, cilantro, lime juice, chutney, mustard, turmeric, cayenne, salt, and pepper. Stir in the shredded chicken, toasted coconut, and diced mango.

Chicken Pot Pie for serves 8 Grown-Ups

4 carrots, peeled and chopped

2 stalks celery, chopped

4 medium red potatoes, peeled and cubed

3/4 pound cremini mushrooms, cleaned with a damp cloth and sliced

1 bay leaf

2 quarts chicken stock

1 large egg, lightly beaten

2 tablespoons water

2 frozen puff pastry sheets (1 box), thawed

4 boneless, skinless chicken breasts

8 tablespoons (1 stick) unsalted butter

1/2 cup all-purpose flour

4 sprigs fresh thyme, leaves stripped and chopped

10 ounces frozen peas, thawed

5 ounces frozen pearl onions, thawed

2 tablespoons Worcestershire sauce

Kosher salt and freshly cracked black pepper, to taste

Chicken pot pie, a dish ostensibly for children, seems to elicit the most excitement from adults. Perhaps it evokes feelings of nostalgia from those of us on the other side of 30, who have fond memories of eating TV dinners while perched in front of the television. Or perhaps we appreciate that chicken pot pie is such a complete meal and ranks up there as one of the best comfort foods of all time. Whatever the reason, you're sure to enjoy this updated, grown-up version of the familiar favorite.

Place the carrots, celery, potatoes, mushrooms, and bay leaf in a Dutch oven or a large, heavy-bottom stockpot and cover with the chicken stock. Bring to a boil then reduce to a gentle simmer until the vegetables are tender, about 15 minutes.

Meanwhile, beat together the egg and 2 table-spoons water in a small bowl. Line a sheet pan with parchment paper. Cut each puff pastry sheet into 4 squares, place on prepared sheet pan, and brush with the egg mixture. Bake according to package directions until puffed and golden brown, 10 to 15 minutes.

Add the chicken breasts to the pot and continue to simmer gently until just cooked through, 10 to 12 minutes. With a slotted spoon, remove the chicken and vegetables to a bowl, reserving the chicken stock in another pot and discarding the bay leaf. Allow the chicken to cool enough to handle.

Wipe out the Dutch oven or stockpot and melt the butter over medium heat, whisk in the flour and thyme to make a roux. Cook for 2 minutes to get rid of the raw flour taste. Slowly and constantly whisk in the chicken stock. Simmer gently for 10 minutes to thicken. Meanwhile, shred or cube the cooled chicken and return it to the pot along with the cooked vegetables, peas, pearl onions, and the Worcestershire sauce. Season with salt and pepper and warm through. Ladle into bowls and top with a puff pastry square.

Lemony Chicken Piccata

serves 4

This is one of those great recipes that serve two purposes: dinner on the table in minutes, and a satisfying release of aggression pounding the chicken breasts flat. Hmmm, therapeutic and delicious!

4   boneless, skinless chicken breasts

1   tablespoon extra-virgin olive oil, plus more for drizzling

Kosher salt and freshly cracked black pepper

1/2   cup all-purpose flour

2   tablespoons unsalted butter

1/2   cup good, dry white wine

Freshly squeezed juice of 1/2 lemon

2   tablespoons capers, drained and rinsed

3   tablespoons chopped fresh flat-leaf parsley, for garnish

Lemon wedges, for garnish

Drizzle the chicken lightly with oil and place between 2 sheets of waxed paper or plastic wrap. Pound the chicken evenly with a meat mallet or rolling pin until 1/4-inch thick. Season the chicken breast with salt and pepper. Place the flour in a shallow dish and dredge the chicken in flour until lightly coated.

Heat 1 tablespoon oil and the butter in a heavy sauté pan over medium-high heat. Shake the excess flour from the chicken and sauté chicken until golden brown, about 3 minutes per side. Remove from the pan and place on a serving platter loosely tented with aluminum foil to keep warm. Add the wine to the pan to deglaze, scraping up any browned bits from the bottom of the pan. Add the lemon juice and capers. Bring the sauce to a bubble for 2 minutes until reduced slightly. Pour the sauce over the chicken. Shower with parsley and serve with lemon wedges.

Orange-Glazed Chicken

serves 4

1/2 cup slivered almonds, for garnish

2 tablespoons extra-virgin olive oil

4 boneless, skinless chicken breasts

Kosher salt and freshly cracked black pepper

1 small onion, chopped

1 (1-inch) piece fresh ginger, peeled and grated

2 cloves garlic, chopped

1 teaspoon chopped fresh thyme

1/2 teaspoon ground cinnamon

1/2 cup chicken stock

3/4 cup good orange marmalade

2 oranges, peeled and sectioned, for garnish

Can one have too many chicken recipes? I don't think so. This is a useful dish to have in your repertoire when you've got dignitaries coming to dinner at a moment's notice. Most of the ingredients you probably have on hand. The pale orange glaze spooned over the chicken, then scattered with almonds and orange sections, is pure art on the plate.

Preheat the oven to 350°F.

Place the almonds in a dry sauté pan and push them around over medium heat until they begin to deepen in color and their nutty aroma begins to waft up under your nose.

Place the oil in a medium sauté pan over medium-high heat and bring almost to the smoking point. Season the chicken with salt and pepper and sear on both sides until golden brown, about 5 minutes per side. Place the chicken on a sheet pan and finish in the oven until just cooked through, 8 to 10 minutes.

Meanwhile, sauté the onion and ginger in the pan drippings until soft and translucent, about 5 minutes. Add the garlic, thyme, and cinnamon and sauté 1 minute. Add the chicken stock and scrape up any brown bits from the bottom of the pan. Whisk in the orange marmalade until smooth and bring up to a boil. Reduce heat and allow the glaze to reduce slightly and thicken. To serve, spoon the sauce over the chicken and garnish with the orange sections and toasted almonds.

A Few Good Eggs
(My Take on the Classic French Omelette) serves 1

I once read that to get a job as a chef in some French restaurants you had to prove you could make a perfect omelette. This is where the job is won or lost. The French take their omelettes very seriously and apply the same care in making them as they do a fancy buerre blanc sauce.

On my personal quest for omelette perfection, I've come upon a few simple truths. 1. The pan matters. A good-quality, ovenproof nonstick skillet, about 9 inches in diameter with curved sides is perfect. 2. Never use more than 3 eggs in your omelette. If you're feeding more than one person, make separate omelettes! 3. You need patience to make a good omelette. You can't rush perfection, so don't try. 4. Season the omelette after you've cooked it, never before. The outside should be perfectly yellow, unmarred by flecks of pepper and free of any brown spots. 5. The omelette should be custard-like and (forgive the expression) as soft as a baby's bottom. 6. An omelette is a beautiful thing, perfect in its simplicity. It needs little more than a scattering of fresh herbs, none of that ham and cheese nonsense. And finally, 7. Julia Child once said, "Wine is essential with anything! Particularly omelettes for lunch." Far be it for me to argue with a master.

3   large eggs

1   tablespoon heavy cream or half-and-half

2   tablespoons unsalted butter, room temperature

    Kosher salt and freshly cracked white pepper, to taste

1   tablespoon finely chopped fresh chives

1   tablespoon finely chopped fresh tarragon

Preheat the oven to 400°F.

Whisk the eggs and cream in a small bowl. In a 9-inch ovenproof nonstick sauté pan, heat the butter over high heat until bubbling and foamy. You want it hot, but whatever you do, don't let it brown. Add the eggs all at once to the center of the pan. There should be an audible hiss. Immediately reduce the heat to low and, using a heat-resistant rubber spatula, stir constantly. The key thing to remember here is, "low and slow." When the eggs begin to just set on the bottom (the top will still be wet) turn off the heat and place the pan in the oven. Cook until the top is still moist-looking and custardlike, about 1 1/2 minutes.

Season with salt and pepper and scatter the chives and tarragon over the top of the eggs. Using the rubber spatula, gently loosen the edge of the eggs from the side of the pan and fold one side over toward the center. Use the pan to help you invert the omelette onto a plate while folding over itself in thirds.

Zucchini-Mushroom Frittata

serves 4

10   basil leaves

8   large eggs

1/4   cup heavy cream

1/2   cup freshly grated Parmesan cheese

     Kosher salt and freshly cracked black pepper

1   tablespoon extra-virgin olive oil

1   tablespoon unsalted butter

1   clove garlic, minced

6   ounces mushrooms, cleaned with a damp cloth and sliced

1   medium zucchini, grated

1   medium tomato, diced, plus more for garnish

For those mornings when I crave something hearty and substantial, but I still want to stick to my low-carb diet, this is my standby. It makes for a satisfying breakfast without sacrificing my dietary virtue.

Preheat the oven to 350°F.

Stack the basil leaves flat, one on top of the other, then roll them lengthwise into a cigar. Thinly slice the leaves into fine ribbons and give them a quick toss to separate. In a large bowl, whisk the eggs and cream together until fluffy. Fold in the basil, reserving some for garnish, and the cheese, salt, and pepper.

In a medium, ovenproof nonstick skillet over medium heat, heat the oil and butter and sauté the garlic, mushrooms, and zucchini until tender, about 6 minutes. Add the tomatoes and sauté, 1 minute. Pour the eggs into the pan and lower the heat so the eggs don't brown. Cook just until the eggs start to set, then place in the oven and bake until golden and puffy, about 10 to 15 minutes. Remove from the pan and cut into wedges. Garnish with the reserved basil and tomatoes. Serve hot or at room temperature.

Honey-Ginger Pork Chops

serves 6

This recipe comes to me by way of a friend whose aunt used to make these pork chops frequently. I admit I was surprised by her use of crystallized ginger in the recipe. If you can't find it, by all means use fresh gingerroot instead. It's just that the crystallized variety adds a sweet heat that in my opinion cannot be duplicated.

1	cup honey
1/2	cup apple cider vinegar
1/4	cup low-sodium soy sauce
4	tablespoons coarsely chopped crystallized ginger
2	cloves garlic, minced
	Freshly cracked black pepper
6	(1-inch-thick) boneless, center-cut pork chops

Combine the honey, vinegar, soy sauce, crystallized ginger, garlic, and pepper in a gallon-size freezer storage bag and add the pork chops. Turn to coat, and refrigerate for 1 to 8 hours.

Preheat the oven to 350°F and heat an indoor grill pan over high heat.

Grill the chops 3 to 4 minutes on each side, brushing with the marinade as they cook. Transfer the chops to a sheet pan and place in the oven to finish cooking until an instant-read thermometer registers 155°F. Allow the pork chops to rest for 5 minutes, loosely tented under a piece of aluminum foil, before serving.

Sidekicks

If you could equate dinner with a movie, and a steak the leading man, the side dish would have to be the supporting actor, right? Though often overlooked and underappreciated, the supporting player can "make" the whole picture. So it is with side dishes. What would fried chicken be without mashed potatoes? Pork chops without applesauce? Eggs without bacon? You get my point. For the times when you just need a little on the side....

Sautéed Mushrooms with Garlic and Thyme

serves 4

8 tablespoons (1 stick) unsalted butter

2 pounds cremini mushrooms, cleaned with a damp cloth and sliced about 1/4 inch thick

2 cloves garlic, minced

4 sprigs fresh thyme, leaves stripped and chopped

Kosher salt and freshly cracked black pepper, to taste

These mushrooms are sophisticated in their simplicity. They are the perfect accompaniment to the Filet Mignon with Blackberry-Cabernet Sauce (page 100).

In a large skillet over medium heat, melt the butter until it begins to bubble. Add the mushrooms, garlic, thyme, salt, and pepper; sauté until the mushrooms are brown and tender, 6 to 7 minutes.

Apricot Couscous

serves 4 to 6

1 1/2 cups chicken stock

1 1/2 cups couscous

1/2 cup diced dried apricots

1 cup diced scallions

1 cup roughly chopped cilantro

Kosher salt and freshly cracked black pepper, to taste

Couscous is one of my favorite side dishes for a number of reasons: It cooks up incredibly fast. I'm talking 5 minutes fast. It goes with everything. It's great hot or at room temperature. The hardest part of making it is boiling the water. And because it's just tiny pasta, it's a blank canvas that will take on any flavor you pair it with.

In a medium saucepan, bring the chicken stock to a boil and immediately stir in the couscous. Turn off the heat and cover the pot. Let the couscous sit until all the liquid is absorbed, about 5 minutes. Fluff the couscous with a fork and transfer to a medium bowl. Stir in the apricots, scallions, and cilantro. Season with salt and pepper. Serve warm or at room temperature.

Herbed Middle Eastern Flat Bread serves 4

2 cloves garlic, minced

1/4 cup extra-virgin olive oil

4 pieces Middle Eastern flat bread, or pita bread

1/4 cup freshly grated Parmesan cheese

1/4 cup chopped mixed herbs (rosemary, thyme, parsley, etc.)

Freshly cracked black pepper, to taste

This is a great alternative to that boring old French bread you've been serving at dinner. Use whatever fresh herbs you have on hand. Great with Easy Hummus (page 45).

Preheat the oven to 400°F.

In a small bowl, combine the garlic with the oil and allow it to steep until the flavor is infused, about 15 minutes. Lay the flat bread out on a sheet pan, brush one side liberally with the oil. Sprinkle the Parmesan cheese and the herbs evenly over the bread. Finish with the pepper, and bake until golden brown and starting to crisp on the edges, 10 to 12 minutes.

Roasted Brussels Sprouts with Crispy Prosciutto

Brussels sprouts have gotten a bad rap over the years. I'm on a mission to change that. These are not the mushy, over-boiled Brussels sprouts you remember from your childhood. They are instead surprisingly sweet and crisp, embellished perfectly with frizzled strips of prosciutto. This may be just the thing that turns you into a sprout lover.

1 1/2   pounds Brussels sprouts

4   tablespoons extra-virgin olive oil

Kosher salt and freshly cracked black pepper, to taste

1/4   pound prosciutto, sliced into thin strips

Freshly squeezed juice of 1 lemon

Preheat the oven to 400°F.

Rinse and trim the woody ends off of the Brussels sprouts. Remove any tough outer leaves. Toss the sprouts in a bowl with 3 tablespoons extra-virgin olive oil, and season with salt and pepper. Tumble onto a sheet pan in a single layer and roast until brown and crisp, 20 to 25 minutes. Give the pan a shake occasionally during cooking, to ensure even color.

Meanwhile, add the remaining 1 tablespoon oil to a sauté pan over medium heat and fry the prosciutto until crisp. Remove from the pan and drain on a paper towel. Remove the pan from the heat and squeeze in the lemon juice, scraping up the brown bits from the bottom of the pan with a wooden spoon. Place the Brussels sprouts in a serving bowl and toss with the pan juices, then shower them with the prosciutto strips. Serve immediately.

Potato Gratin

serves to 8

I was shocked to learn that classic French potato gratin doesn't have any cheese in it! Had my mother been bamboozling me all these years? Well, not exactly. Most people think of potato gratin and American scalloped potatoes as being one and the same. They aren't. Scalloped potatoes almost always have cheese in them and are sometimes embellished with other ingredients such as onions or ham. Whether or not to add cheese to a potato gratin is the subject of great debate. For the gratin purists out there, the answer is a resounding "no!" I have come to agree. The miracle of this gratin is that it somehow develops a wonderful cheesy creaminess without any cheese at all. Like all miracles, it defies logic and explanation.

4   tablespoons (1/2 stick) **unsalted butter, room temperature**

1   scant cup whole milk

1   large clove garlic, crushed

3/4   teaspoon kosher salt

1/2   teaspoon freshly ground white pepper

1/8   teaspoon freshly grated nutmeg

11/2   pounds russet potatoes

11/2   cups heavy cream

Preheat the oven to 425°F.

Use 2 tablespoons butter to liberally butter the bottom of a 5 to 6 cup metal gratin dish. (I have also successfully used a 9x13 inch metal baking pan like one you would bake brownies in. Both pans produce a great crust underneath the potatoes. Pyrex would do in a pinch, but it's not my preferred choice.)

Place a small saucepan with the milk, garlic, salt, white pepper, and nutmeg, over low heat. Meanwhile, peel the potatoes, then slice them to about a 1/8-inch thickness, discarding the smallest slices. (A mandolin is perfect for this, but I usually opt for a really sharp butcher knife.) Do not wash the potatoes after slicing them, as the surface starch is indispensable.

Evenly arrange the potatoes in the bottom of the baking pan, one overlapping row at a time. Layer each row about a third of the way over the previous row. Continue until the baking pan is neatly paved. It should look something like a shingled rooftop.

Increase the heat under the milk and bring to a boil; remove from heat. Fish out the garlic clove and pour the milk over the potatoes. Cover the pan with aluminum foil and bake in the middle of the oven until most of the milk has been absorbed, about 15 minutes. Meanwhile, set the cream over low heat and bring to a boil. Pour the cream over the semi-cooked potatoes and dot the entire surface with the remaining 2 tablespoons butter.

Return the potatoes to the oven and bake, uncovered, until the potatoes are golden brown and spotted with darker, crisp areas, 20 to 25 minutes. The potatoes will be dotted with thickened cream, especially between the slices. Allow the gratin to rest for 10 minutes before serving.

Perfect Mashed Potatoes

I know it seems weird to give a recipe for mashed potatoes, but there are as many ways to make them as there are to peel them. And, by the way, I don't peel mine. Partly out of laziness, but mostly because I love the flavor and rustic texture the skins give. I mash these by hand with an old-fashioned potato masher, just like the one grandma used.

Scrub the potatoes and cut into rough and tumble chunks of about the same size (so that they cook evenly). Place in a large stockpot or Dutch oven and cover with cold water. Bring to a boil and generously salt the water. Reduce heat to a simmer and cook until the potatoes are fork-tender, 20 to 25 minutes. Drain the potatoes and tumble into a large bowl. Add the butter, sour cream, salt, and pepper. Mash the potatoes to desired texture. Taste for seasonings and dig in.

2   large baking potatoes

Kosher salt and freshly cracked black pepper, to taste

4   tablespoons (1/2 stick) unsalted butter, room temperature

1/2   cup sour cream, or to taste

126 BOY EATS WORLD!

Warm Fennel and Parmesan Salad

Fennel is a beautiful, pale green bulb that is widely available yet completely underappreciated and underutilized by a lot of home cooks. It's related to both carrots and parsnips, but it has a mild licorice-y flavor entirely its own. Grilling enhances that flavor, while bringing out a hidden sweetness. Paired here with a nutty, salty Parmesan and brightened up with a bit of fresh lemon juice, it's a winning combination.

2   large fennel bulbs, tops removed

      Extra-virgin olive oil, for drizzling

      Kosher salt and freshly cracked black pepper, to taste

4   ounces Parmesan cheese, shaved with a peeler

      Freshly squeezed juice of 1 lemon

      Handful of hand-torn, fresh flat-leaf parsley

Preheat a grill pan or outdoor grill over high heat.

Trim the tops off of the fennel bulbs and cut bulbs into quarters, leaving the core intact. Drizzle the fennel with the oil to lightly coat; season with salt and pepper. Grill the fennel until charred grill marks appear on all sides and it begins to get tender, about 4 minutes per side. Remove to a cutting board and allow to cool enough to handle comfortably.

Place the fennel quarters on their sides and cut into them on an angle to remove the core; discard. Slice into thin strips and place in a medium bowl. Add the shaved Parmesan, lemon juice, and parsley and toss lightly to combine. Feel free to add another drizzle of oil and more salt and pepper if you think it needs it.

Roasted Artichokes with Sun-Dried Tomato Aioli

serves 4

FOR THE AIOLI

1 head garlic

Extra-virgin olive oil, for drizzling

Kosher salt and freshly cracked black pepper, to taste

1/4 cup oil-packed sun-dried tomatoes, drained

1 tablespoon freshly squeezed lemon juice

2 cups mayonnaise

FOR THE ARTICHOKES

1 quart water

Freshly squeezed juice of 2 lemons

1/2 cup good white wine

3 tablespoons extra-virgin olive oil

2 bay leaves

4 cloves garlic, smashed with the side of a knife

Kosher salt and freshly cracked black pepper, to taste

4 large artichokes

1/2 lemon

FOR THE VINAIGRETTE

1/4 cup freshly squeezed lemon juice

3/4 cup extra-virgin olive oil

Kosher salt and freshly cracked black pepper, to taste

Preheat the oven to 400°F.

To make the aioli, first roast the garlic: Slice 1/3 off of the top of the head of garlic to expose the cloves. Drizzle with a bit of oil, season with salt and pepper, and wrap loosely in a piece of aluminum foil. Roast until the garlic is soft and the top begins to caramelize and ooze a bit, about 45 minutes. Remove and let cool to room temperature.

To prepare the artichokes, place the water, lemon juice, wine, oil, bay leaves, and garlic in a covered pot large enough to hold the artichokes. Season the liquid generously with salt and pepper and bring to a simmer.

Cut the stems off the artichokes close to the base so the artichokes stand upright. Remove any small tough leaves at the bottom and discard. Cut off the top 1 inch of the artichoke with a serrated knife and trim the spiky tops off of the remaining leaves with kitchen shears. Rub the cut surfaces of the artichoke with the lemon half to keep them from discoloring. Place the artichokes upright in the liquid and cover. Steam until a sharp knife can be inserted easily into the bases, about 30 minutes.

Meanwhile, continue to make the aioli. Take 3 cloves from the roasted head of garlic and save the rest for another use. Squeeze the roasted garlic out from the skins. Place the tomatoes, lemon juice, and garlic in a blender and blend until smooth. Add the mayonnaise and blend once more to combine. Season with salt and pepper.

When the artichokes are done, remove with tongs and allow them to drain on paper towels until cool enough to handle. Separate the leaves slightly with your thumbs and pull out the purple and yellow leaves from the center until you've exposed the fuzzy choke. With a spoon, carefully scrape out the choke, creating a cavity in the center. Place the artichokes upright on a sheet pan.

Preheat the broiler.

To make the vinaigrette, whisk together the lemon juice and oil. Season with salt and pepper and drizzle lightly inside and over the artichokes. Place them under the broiler just until the edges of the leaves begin to crisp, 1 to 2 minutes. Serve warm or cold with the aioli.

Artichokes are one of those vegetables that people truly fear, or at least get really intimidated by. I know they look scary, all prickly and tough, but really they are incredibly tender-bellied and delicious. Once you know how to deal with them, the possibilities are endless. I love them with the Sun-Dried Tomato Aioli, or just dipped in melted butter.

Mango and Black Bean Salsa

serves 4

2 fresh mangos, peeled, pitted, and diced

1/2 red bell pepper, diced

1/2 jalapeño pepper, seeded and minced

1/2 hothouse cucumber, chopped

1/2 of a 14-ounce can black beans, drained and rinsed

Freshly squeezed juice of 2 limes

Kosher salt and freshly cracked black pepper, to taste

2 tablespoons chopped fresh cilantro

This recipe is very "California Cuisine," but not at all fussy or pretentious. It's cool and refreshing and a great pairing with Sweet and Spicy Glazed Salmon (page 76).

In a medium bowl combine the mango, red bell pepper, jalapeño, cucumber, black beans, lime juice, salt, and pepper. Stir in the chopped cilantro and allow the flavors to develop for 30 minutes at room temperature.

Twice-Baked Potatoes

serves 4

As far as I'm concerned, this is potato nirvana. You have the best thing about a baked potato (that perfectly crispy skin) and the best thing about mashed potatoes (that fluffy, buttery pulp)—topped with cheese and bacon. This is one of the dreamiest combinations in the world.

- 4 large russet potatoes
- 4 tablespoons (1/2 stick) unsalted butter, room temperature
- 1/2 cup sour cream
- 2 scallions, finely chopped
- 1/8 teaspoon freshly grated nutmeg, or to taste

  Kosher salt and freshly cracked black pepper, to taste
- 1/2 cup shredded sharp cheddar cheese
- 4 strips bacon, cooked and crumbled (1/4 cup), for garnish
- 2 tablespoons chopped fresh flat-leaf parsley, for garnish

Preheat the oven to 400°F.

Scrub the potatoes and dry well. Pierce the skin in several places with a fork and place directly on the rack in the center of the oven. Bake until tender, 45 minutes to 1 hour. Allow the potatoes to rest until cool enough to handle, about 10 minutes.

Holding each potato carefully with a kitchen towel, cut a slit down its entire length and carefully scoop out most of the potato pulp into a medium bowl, being careful to leave enough potato in the skin so the shells hold up, about 1/4 inch. Mash the potato pulp lightly with the butter and sour cream. Stir in the scallions, nutmeg, salt, and pepper.

Refill the shells with the mashed potato mixture, mounding it slightly. Sprinkle the cheese and bacon on top of the potatoes and place them on a sheet pan; return to the oven and bake until heated through, about 15 minutes. Remove from oven, shower with the chopped parsley, and serve immediately.

Aunt Judi's Dinner Rolls

makes about 40 rolls

I have many fond memories associated with these rolls. They were my aunt Judi's specialty, and we simply couldn't have a family gathering without them. If the idea of making your own dinner rolls seems improbable and quaint, let me say this: You're depriving yourself of the fun and satisfaction that making, kneading, and playing with bread dough provides. The end result is a tender roll, all yeasty and light, the perfect accompaniment to any meal. Served warm and slathered with butter, there is nothing better.

1 1/2   cups warm water (about 110°F)

3/4   cup sugar, plus 1 teaspoon

2   tablespoons active dry yeast

2   sticks butter, melted, plus more for brushing tops

2   teaspoons kosher salt

1   cup boiling water

7   to 9 1/2 cups all-purpose flour

4   large eggs, lightly beaten

   Nonstick butter-flavored cooking spray

In a small mixing bowl, bloom the yeast: Pour 1/2 cup of the warm water and a teaspoon of sugar over the yeast and let it sit until foamy, about 10 minutes.

Meanwhile, in the bowl of a freestanding mixer fitted with a dough hook, combine the melted butter, 3/4 cup sugar, salt, and boiling water. Add 6 cups of the flour and mix on low speed. Add the bloomed yeast mixture and combine well. With the mixer still on low speed, add the eggs a little at a time until combined. Add 1 more cup of flour, and slowly pour in the remaining 1 cup warm water. At this point, the dough will most likely be very wet, loose, and sticky. Slowly mix in up to 2 1/2 cups more flour until the dough is soft and not too sticky. My aunt Judi calls it "pokey." Cover the bowl with a clean kitchen towel and let the dough rise in a warm place until doubled in size, about 45 minutes. (My aunt would turn the oven on to 300°F and turn it off after one minute.)

Line a sheet pan with parchment paper and spray with nonstick butter-flavored cooking spray. Set aside.

Punch the dough down and roll it into little balls, roughly the size of a golf ball. Use a little flour if they stick to your hands. Place the rolls on the prepared pan with their sides touching slightly. Cover loosely with a kitchen towel and set aside to rise again until doubled in size, about 45 minutes.

Preheat the oven to 375°F.

Brush the tops of the rolls with melted butter and bake until beautifully browned, 15 to 20 minutes.

Old-Fashioned Herb and Cheese Biscuits

makes **18** biscuits

These are the kind of country biscuits my grandma used to make for everything from breakfast to dinner. I no longer have her exact recipe, but this comes pretty close.

3¹/2   cups all-purpose flour, plus more for dusting

2   teaspoons baking powder

1   teaspoon baking soda

1   teaspoon kosher salt

1   cup cold unsalted butter, cut into small pieces

1   cup grated sharp cheddar cheese

2   tablespoons finely chopped fresh flat-leaf parsley

2   scallions, minced

1¹/4   cups buttermilk, plus more if needed

1   large egg, beaten

2   tablespoons milk

Preheat the oven to 400°F.

Line a sheet pan with parchment paper and set aside. In a large bowl, whisk together the flour, baking powder, baking soda, and salt. With a pastry blender, your hands, or an electric mixer set on low, cut in the butter until the mixture resembles coarse cornmeal. Stir in the cheese, parsley, and scallions. Stir in the buttermilk with a fork until a dough forms (add more buttermilk, a little at a time, if too dry).

Place the dough on a lightly floured surface and shape it into a ball (do not overwork dough). Pat it out to a ³/4-inch thickness. Using a floured 2¹/2-inch biscuit cutter or an inverted glass of the same size, cut out the biscuits and transfer to the prepared sheet pan. Reroll the scraps and cut out more biscuits.

Mix together the egg and milk. Brush the biscuit tops with the egg wash. Bake until golden brown, 15 to 18 minutes. Remove from oven and serve immediately.

Brown Rice Salad with Asparagus and Mint

serves 6

I never thought I'd be excited about brown rice, until now. I'm constantly faced with the challenge of coming up with inventive dishes to keep my clients happy and eating healthy. This recipe came about as a way to jazz up yet another bowl of the stuff.

2   cups California short-grain brown rice

3   cups chicken stock

1   bunch asparagus, chopped into 1-inch pieces

1   teaspoon sugar

1   tablespoon grated fresh ginger

Grated zest and freshly squeezed juice of 1 lime

1/2   cup chopped fresh mint

1/2   cup chopped scallions

Kosher salt and freshly cracked black pepper, to taste

Cook the rice according to package directions, using chicken stock in place of water. Place the asparagus in the pot for the last 3 minutes of cooking, to lightly steam. Fluff the rice with a fork and stir in the sugar, ginger, lime zest and juice, mint, scallions, salt, and pepper. Serve warm or at room temperature.

Lemon-Mint Peas

serves 4

8 tablespoons (1 stick) unsalted butter, room temperature

1 tablespoon freshly squeezed lemon juice

1/4 teaspoon grated lemon zest

4 cups frozen peas

2 tablespoons chopped fresh mint leaves, for garnish

Peas are one of the few vegetables I actually prefer to use frozen. The reason? Peas are picked at the peak of their freshness and flash frozen. They're usually much better than the ones you'll find in your supermarket produce section, even in season.

Using the back of a spoon, cream together the butter, lemon juice, and zest. Tumble the peas into a medium-size saucepan and combine with the butter mixture. Cook over gentle heat, just until the butter is melted and the peas are heated through. Shower with fresh mint and serve.

Red-Onion Marmalade

makes 2 cups

1 tablespoon extra-virgin olive oil

4 medium red onions, sliced into thin rings

3 tablespoons balsamic vinegar

1 tablespoon light brown sugar

1/2 teaspoon grated orange zest

2 tablespoons freshly squeezed orange juice

1 teaspoon kosher salt

This sweet-and-sour onion marmalade is the perfect thing to dress up grilled chicken, salmon, even steak! Serve warm or cold. It can be made a week in advance and refrigerated until serving time.

In large skillet, heat the oil over low heat. Add the onions and cook, stirring frequently until soft, about 15 minutes.

Stir in the vinegar, brown sugar, orange zest, orange juice, and salt. Cook, stirring frequently, until glossy, about 15 minutes. Serve warm, at room temperature, or chilled.

Broccoli with Lemony Breadcrumbs

serves 6

This is a quick and simple way to perk up ordinary broccoli and take it to another level.

2 large bunches fresh broccoli, cut into florets

6 tablespoons unsalted butter

1 cup dried plain breadcrumbs

Grated zest of 2 lemons

Freshly squeezed juice of 1 lemon

Kosher salt and freshly cracked black pepper, to taste

Pour about 1 inch water into a large pot with a cover and put a steamer basket in the pot. Bring the water to a simmer. Place the broccoli in the steamer basket and steam until crisp-tender, about 3 minutes.

Meanwhile, melt the butter in a small sauté pan over medium heat and sauté the bread crumbs until golden and toasted. Sprinkle the lemon zest and juice over the breadcrumbs. Season with salt and pepper and stir constantly until the breadcrumbs are dry. Sprinkle over the broccoli and serve immediately.

Compound Butters

makes just over 1/2 cup each

LEMON-PARSLEY BUTTER

8 tablespoons (1 stick) unsalted butter, room temperature

2 tablespoons freshly squeezed lemon juice

1 teaspoon grated lemon zest

3 tablespoons finely chopped fresh flat-leaf parsley

Kosher salt and white pepper, to taste

Compound butters are a culinary revelation! I can scarcely remember a time without them. They're incredibly easy and fast to make. They last for months in your freezer (a thought I find tremendously comforting), and the flavor combinations are endless. The following suggestions just graze the surface of possibility. A pat of flavored butter is just the thing on a piece of grilled chicken, fish, steak, vegetables, or toasted bread.

TARRAGON BUTTER

8 tablespoons (1 stick) unsalted butter, room temperature

1/4 cup finely chopped fresh tarragon leaves

Kosher salt and white pepper, to taste

GORGONZOLA BUTTER

8 tablespoons (1 stick) unsalted butter, room temperature

1 clove garlic, grated or put through a garlic press

4 ounces Gorgonzola cheese, crumbled, room temperature

2 tablespoons finely chopped fresh flat-leaf parsley

Kosher salt and white pepper, to taste

GARLIC BUTTER

8 tablespoons (1 stick) unsalted butter, room temperature

3 cloves garlic, grated or put through a garlic press

2 tablespoons finely chopped fresh flat-leaf parsley

Kosher salt and white pepper, to taste

In a medium mixing bowl, combine all ingredients and mix together with a rubber spatula. Or combine in a food processor. Scrape the butter onto a long sheet of wax paper, forming a straight line. Fold the end of the paper over the butter and roll into an even cylinder, about the diameter of a silver dollar. Twist each end and place in the refrigerator until solid, about 2 hours.

For long-term storage, keep in the freezer. Remove needed amount when ready to use, and allow to soften to room temperature for easy spreading.

PARSLEY-DILL-LEMON BUTTER

8 tablespoons (1 stick) unsalted butter, room temperature

2 tablespoons freshly squeezed lemon juice

1 teaspoon grated lemon zest

2 tablespoons finely chopped fresh flat-leaf parsley

2 tablespoons finely chopped fresh dill

Kosher salt and white pepper, to taste

CILANTRO-LIME-CHIPOTLE BUTTER

8 tablespoons (1 stick) unsalted butter, room temperature

2 tablespoons freshly squeezed lime juice

2 tablespoons finely chopped cilantro

1 teaspoon grated lime zest

1 teaspoon chipotle powder, or to taste

Kosher salt and white pepper, to taste

Childhood Favorites

Because my love of cooking began in childhood, I thought it only appropriate to include a few of my favorites from that time. The food in this chapter is decidedly unpretentious. It is the kind of food I loved eating as child. The kind of food I still love eating as an adult, and whip up for myself when I am in need of comfort. Although I am loath to use the word casserole, some of these recipes are just that and should be appreciated for their retro, kitsch quality and the feeling of nostalgia they elicit. There's no doubt in my mind that your kids will enjoy these dishes, and you may find, as I have, that these recipes reach far beyond childhood.

Chocolate No-Bake Cookies

makes 12 large cookies

8 tablespoons (1 stick) unsalted butter, room temperature

2 cups sugar

1/2 cup milk

5 tablespoons unsweetened cocoa

3/4 cups chunky peanut butter*

1 tablespoon pure vanilla extract

3 cups quick-cooking oats

These may not be the most attractive cookies you will ever eat—in fact, they're downright crude looking—but I promise you they will be among the most delicious you've ever tasted. Although they're very easy to throw together, there are a couple of important things you must do to ensure success every time. First, make sure to use the quick-cooking one-minute oats. Second, once you bring the mixture to a boil, it's critical that you only boil it for one minute! Otherwise, the finished product will be dry and crumbly, resulting in a less-than-perfect cookie. Having said that, I confess that rarely in my childhood did these cookies make it to the "perfect" stage. They were usually devoured greedily with a spoon right off the wax paper, or out of the pan long before they had a chance to set up.

In a large saucepan or Dutch oven over high heat, combine the butter, sugar, milk, and cocoa. Stir together until melted and smooth. Bring to a boil for exactly 1 minute. Remove from the heat and quickly whisk in the peanut butter, vanilla, and oatmeal. Drop heaping spoonfuls onto waxed paper and allow the cookies to cool and set completely, about 10 minutes.

*I use chunky peanut butter because I like the crunch and texture. Feel free to use smooth if you prefer.

Swedish Cookies

This is my all-time favorite Christmas cookie! I don't know exactly where the recipe came from, and to be perfectly honest, I don't even know if they're Swedish. My mom tells me this cookie has been in our family as long as she can remember. My grandma used to make them every year and I swear I used to start thinking about these buttery, crispy gems in August!

makes about 50 cookies

To make the dough, cream together the butter and cream cheese in the bowl of a freestanding mixer fitted with a paddle attachment or with a handheld electric mixer. Slowly add the flour, a little at a time, mixing on low speed until incorporated and just starting to come together. Turn the dough out onto a board dusted with confectioners' sugar and knead a few times. Divide the dough into 4 equal parts and form each part into a ball; wrap each ball in plastic wrap. Place in the refrigerator to chill for 1 hour.

Meanwhile, make the filling. Whip the egg whites in the bowl of a freestanding mixer fitted with a whisk attachment, or with an electric beater, until foamy and able to hold a soft peak. Gently fold in the sugar and the walnuts. The mixture will be thick and dense.

Preheat the oven to 350°F.

Line a baking sheet with parchment paper. Generously dust a board with confectioners' sugar. Working with one chilled ball of dough at a time, roll the dough into a 1/4-inch-thick rectangle. Using a sharp knife, cut the dough into approximately 2 1/2-inch squares. I do this freehand; don't worry about making them perfect. Place a teaspoon-size dollop of filling in the center of each square and pinch the two opposite corners together. The scraps of dough can be gathered up, chilled, and rerolled. Transfer the cookies to the prepared pan and place in the refrigerator to chill, 10 minutes. Transfer to the oven and bake until golden brown and crisp, 15 to 20 minutes. Let cool on a rack before serving.

FOR THE DOUGH

- 1 pound (4 sticks) unsalted butter, room temperature
- 1 pound cream cheese, room temperature
- 4 cups all-purpose flour

  Confectioners' sugar, for dusting

FOR THE FILLING

- 3 large egg whites, lightly beaten
- 3 cups sugar
- 3 cups finely chopped walnuts

Peanut Butter Crisscrosses

makes 5 dozen cookies

A peanut butter cookie is a wonderful thing. So perfect in its simplicity, it needs no further introduction.

2 sticks unsalted butter, room temperature

1 cup granulated sugar

1 cup packed light brown sugar

1 cup chunky peanut butter*

2 large eggs

1 teaspoon pure vanilla extract

3 cups all-purpose flour

2 teaspoons baking soda

1/2 teaspoon kosher salt

Preheat the oven to 350°F.

Line a baking sheet with parchment paper. In the bowl of a freestanding mixer fitted with a paddle attachment or a handheld electric mixer, cream together the butter, both sugars, and the peanut butter. Add in the eggs one at a time, scraping down the sides of the bowl as needed. Add the vanilla and mix until well incorporated.

In a medium bowl, whisk together the flour, baking soda, and salt and add to the wet ingredients with the mixer on low speed, mixing until the dough forms.

Roll the dough into balls about the size of a walnut and place 2 inches apart on the prepared pan. Dip a fork in flour and, using the back of the tines, flatten the balls to about 1/2 inch thick, making a crisscross pattern across the cookies. Bake until lightly golden brown on the edges, 10 to 12 minutes. Let cool on a rack before serving.

*I use chunky peanut butter because I like the crunch and texture. Feel free to use smooth if you prefer.

Oatmeal Chocolate Chip Cookies

Oatmeal cookies probably don't sound very exciting to you. They usually don't to me either, but I love this particular cookie for two reasons. For one, I love the combination of cinnamon and chocolate, and two, because there is milk in the dough, these cookies stay incredibly soft and chewy. Feel free to use raisins if you prefer, but I look for any excuse to add chocolate to my life.

2 sticks unsalted butter, room temperature

1 cup sugar

2 large eggs

2 teaspoons pure vanilla extract

6 tablespoons milk

2 cups all-purpose flour

1 teaspoon kosher salt

1 teaspoon baking soda

1 teaspoon baking powder

2 teaspoons cinnamon

2 cups old-fashioned oatmeal

1 (12-ounce) package semi-sweet chocolate chips

Preheat the oven to 375°F.

Line a baking sheet with parchment paper. In the bowl of a freestanding mixer fitted with a paddle attachment or with a handheld electric mixer, cream together the butter and sugar. Add in the eggs one at a time, scraping down the sides of the bowl as needed. Add the vanilla and milk and mix until well incorporated.

In a medium bowl, whisk together the flour, salt, baking soda, baking powder, and cinnamon. Stir in the oatmeal. With the mixer on low speed, add the dry ingredients to the wet ingredients, mixing until the dough comes together. Fold in the chocolate chips using a wooden spoon or rubber spatula so as not to break them up or melt the chocolate with the heat of the mixer. Drop the dough by the rounded spoonful (or use a small ice cream scoop) onto the prepared pan and bake until golden brown on the edges, 10 to 12 minutes. Let cool on a rack before serving.

Old-Fashioned Carrot Cake

serves 12

Truth be told, I don't much care for carrots on their own. Bake them into a cake however, with tons of gooey cream cheese frosting, and I can eat them all day long. Somehow I don't think this is quite what my mother had in mind when she said, "Eat your vegetables!"

FOR THE CAKE

2 tablespoons unsalted butter, room temperature, for pans

2 cups all-purpose flour, plus more for pans

4 large eggs

2 cups sugar

1/4 cup vegetable oil

1 teaspoon pure vanilla extract

2 teaspoons baking soda

2 teaspoons cinnamon

1 teaspoon kosher salt

3 cups shredded carrots

1 cup raisins

1 cup chopped walnuts

FOR THE FROSTING

2 sticks unsalted butter, room temperature

2 (8-ounce) packages cream cheese, room temperature

1 1/2 teaspoons pure vanilla extract

1 pound confectioners' sugar, sifted

Preheat the oven to 350°F.

Butter and flour two 9-inch cake rounds, or one 13x9x2-inch glass baking dish.

To make the cake, in the bowl of a freestanding mixer fitted with a paddle attachment or with a handheld electric mixer, mix together the eggs, sugar, vegetable oil, and vanilla.

In a medium bowl, whisk together the flour, baking soda, cinnamon, and salt. Stir the dry ingredients into the wet and fold in the carrots, raisins, and walnuts by hand. Pour the batter into the prepared pan(s) and bake until a toothpick inserted in the middle comes out clean, 30 to 45 minutes. Let cool completely on a rack before removing from pan(s).

To make the frosting, cream together the butter and cream cheese in a medium bowl. Add the vanilla and confectioners' sugar and whip with an electric mixer until fluffy and smooth. When the cake is completely cool, slather the frosting all over the cake and cut into big chunks. My idea of heaven.

Snickerdoodles

makes about 20 cookies

However ridiculous the name, I include these cookies here without embarrassment. They were a staple in my house growing up, and to this day, the mere mention of a snickerdoodle makes me smile.

2   sticks unsalted butter, room temperature

1 1/2 cups sugar, plus 2 teaspoons

2   large eggs

1   teaspoon pure vanilla extract

2 3/4 cups all-purpose flour

2   teaspoons cream of tartar

1   teaspoon baking soda

1/2   teaspoon kosher salt

2   teaspoons ground cinnamon

In the bowl of a freestanding mixer fitted with a paddle attachment or with a handheld electric mixer, cream together the butter and 1 1/2 cups sugar. Add in the eggs one at a time, scraping down the sides of the bowl as needed. Add the vanilla and mix until well incorporated.

In a medium bowl, whisk together the flour, cream of tartar, baking soda, and salt. With the mixer on low speed, add the dry ingredients to the wet ingredients, mixing until the dough comes together. Cover the bowl with plastic wrap and place in the refrigerator to chill for 1 hour.

Preheat the oven to 350°F.

Line a sheet pan with parchment paper. In a small bowl, stir together the cinnamon and the remaining 2 teaspoons sugar. Roll the dough into balls about the size of a walnut and coat each one in the cinnamon sugar. Place on the prepared pan about 2 inches apart and bake until puffed, lightly golden, and cracked on the top, 10 to 12 minutes.

Shipwreck Stew

serves 6

2 tablespoons extra-virgin olive oil

1 medium onion, roughly chopped

1 pound lean ground beef

1 teaspoon chopped fresh thyme

Kosher salt and freshly cracked black pepper

2 medium-size russet potatoes, peeled and cubed

1 (14-ounce) can kidney beans, undrained

1 (10-ounce) can Campbell's condensed tomato soup

6 slices center-cut bacon

As a kid with an overactive imagination, I reveled in tales of shipwrecked pirates eating this hearty, simple stew made from what they had on hand. I suppose it was just some clever story my mom invented to get me to eat dinner. All I know is, it worked. These days, I'll pair this with a green salad and a glass of red wine for a complete grown-up meal.

Preheat the oven to 375°F.

Heat the oil in a large sauté pan over medium-high heat. Add the onion and sauté until they begin to soften, about 5 minutes. Add the ground beef and thyme and season generously with salt and pepper. Taste for seasonings and drain off any excess fat.

Meanwhile, place the cubed potatoes in a single layer in the bottom of a 4-quart covered casserole dish. Pour the undrained kidney beans over the potatoes, then add the meat and onion mixture. Top the whole thing with the tomato soup, making sure to go all the way to the edge to form a seal. Lay the bacon slices over the top. Bake for 30 minutes, covered, then remove the lid and cook until the whole thing is bubbling, the bacon is crisp, and the potatoes are tender when a knife is inserted in the middle, 20 to 25 minutes.

Sticky Orange Juice Cake

serves 12 to 15

It's a fallacy to think that chefs, when they cook at home anyway, make everything from scratch. When you spend all day, everyday, cooking in a professional kitchen, you learn to take a few shortcuts wherever you can. But only, of course, if the finished result is delicious. What makes this cake special is the glaze you pour over the top, while it's still warm from the oven. It's moist and delicately orangey. Go ahead, open up a box of cake mix.

FOR THE CAKE

- 1   package lemon cake mix
- 1   (3-ounce) package instant lemon pudding mix
- 3/4   cup water
- 3/4   cup vegetable oil
- 4   large eggs

FOR THE GLAZE

- 2   cups confectioners' sugar, sifted
- 2   tablespoons unsalted butter, melted
- 2   tablespoons water
- 1/2   cup freshly squeezed orange juice

Preheat the oven to 350°F.

In the bowl of a freestanding mixer fitted with a whisk attachment, combine the cake mix with the pudding mix, water, oil, and eggs. Beat at medium speed for 2 minutes, scraping down the sides as needed, until the batter is smooth. Bake in an ungreased 13x9-inch baking pan until a toothpick inserted in the center of the cake comes out clean, 30 minutes.

Meanwhile, to make the glaze, whisk the confectioners' sugar with the melted butter, water, and orange juice in a small bowl until smooth; set aside.

When the cake comes out of the oven, allow it to cool, 10 minutes. Poke the entire surface with the tines of a fork, about every inch or so. Pour the glaze evenly over the top, allowing it to soak into the cake. Cool completely and cut into big delicious chunks.

Egg Salad Sandwiches

serves 2

I'm something of a purist when it comes to egg salad. I like mine simple, not a lot of clutter, just a bit of celery for crunch. That way, the egg really shines through, becomes the main ingredient. You'll notice I don't use any mustard in my recipe—though feel free to add some if you prefer.

4	eggs
1/2	cup chopped celery
1/4	cup mayonnaise
	Kosher salt and freshly cracked black pepper, to taste
4	slices rustic wheat bread

Place the eggs in a medium saucepan and fill with enough cold water to completely submerge them. Place over high heat and bring the water to a boil. Turn off the heat and cover the saucepan with a tight-fitting lid. Let the eggs hang out for exactly 15 minutes. Drain and run cold water over them.*

Peel and roughly chop the eggs into manageable pieces and tumble them into a small bowl. Add the celery to the eggs. Glob in the mayonnaise, along with plenty of salt and pepper. Stir gently to combine, and dole out between 2 slices of bread, topping with the remaining 2 slices, for an absolutely perfect lunch.

*I don't mean to insult your intelligence by including instructions on how to boil an egg, but there is an art to it. That is, if you don't want to end up with a rubbery yolk with that grayish-green ring around it. Overcooking or "over boiling," in this case, is the biggest mistake people make. It doesn't take 20 minutes to boil an egg! So, for everyone out there who's ever wondered how to boil the perfect egg, here's the answer.

Easy Bean and Bacon Soup

serves 4 to 6

When I was a kid, my favorite variety of Campbell's soup was Bean with Bacon. That same flavor combination of salty bacon and creamy beans is the inspiration for this grown-up, stick-to-your-ribs version of my childhood favorite.

4   strips center-cut bacon, chopped

1   medium onion, chopped

1   large carrot, peeled and chopped

2   stalks celery, chopped

4   cloves garlic, chopped

2   (15-ounce) cans cannelini or great Northern beans, drained

2   to 4 cups chicken stock

2   tablespoons roughly chopped fresh flat-leaf parsley

Kosher salt and freshly cracked black pepper, to taste

In a large Dutch oven or heavy-bottom stockpot over medium heat, fry the bacon until crisp. Remove and drain on a paper towel. Add the onion, carrot, and celery to the pan drippings and sauté until the vegetables begin to soften, 5 to 6 minutes. Add the garlic and sauté for 1 minute more. Add the beans and 2 cups chicken stock; bring to a boil. Cover and reduce heat; simmer, 10 minutes. With a potato masher or a fork, partially mash the bean mixture until the soup thickens slightly. I like to leave several of the beans whole for texture. Thin the soup out with additional chicken stock if necessary. Stir in the reserved bacon and the parsley. Season with salt and pepper and serve immediately.

My Mom's Fried Chicken

serves 6

I like fried chicken with character. That means chicken with that really crispy, thick crust on the outside and incredibly moist, tender meat on the inside. The way to achieve that perfect crust is by dipping the chicken, first in the flour, then in the buttermilk, then in the flour again. With its contrast in textures, this chicken is pretty much culinary perfection.

2 (3-pound) frying chickens, each cut into 8 pieces

1 quart buttermilk

1 tablespoon freshly squeezed lemon juice

2 cups all-purpose flour

1 tablespoon garlic powder

1 tablespoon kosher salt

1 tablespoon freshly cracked black pepper

1 teaspoon dried thyme

1 teaspoon dried oregano

1 teaspoon Hungarian sweet paprika

Vegetable oil, for frying

Place the chicken pieces in a large bowl and pour in the buttermilk and lemon juice; submerge the chicken. Cover with plastic wrap and place in the refrigerator. Allow the chicken to soak for at least 3 hours; overnight is best.

Meanwhile, in a gallon-size plastic freezer bag or a shallow baking dish, combine the flour, garlic powder, salt, pepper, thyme, oregano, and paprika. Mix well. Remove the chicken pieces from the buttermilk, drain well and pat dry with paper towels. Coat the chicken pieces, a few at a time, in the seasoned flour, then quickly plunge them back into the buttermilk, and once more in the flour. Place on a wire rack to dry, 15 minutes.

Pour 2 inches oil into a deep, heavy-bottom frying pan or Dutch oven; heat the oil over high heat until it registers 375°F on a deep-fry thermometer. As soon as you add the chicken, the temperature of the oil will drop significantly. Adjust the heat to maintain oil temperature.

Preheat the oven to 350°F.

Using tongs, place the chicken carefully into the hot oil. Work in batches and be careful not to overcrowd the pan. Fry the chicken until golden brown, 4 to 5 minutes per side. Drain on paper towels then place on a sheet pan. Place the pan in the oven and bake, turning the pieces halfway through, until the chicken is no longer pink inside, 30 to 35 minutes. Serve immediately with lots of Perfect Mashed Potatoes (page 126).

Aunt Harriett's Macaroni Salad

If there is anything that competes with mashed potatoes as my all-time favorite comfort food, this would be it. And my aunt Harriett's recipe is the best. Like all good home cooks, she never really measures anything. Rather, she throws in a pinch of this and a dash of that until she gets it right. So don't get hung up on exact measurements. There's something liberating about tossing things freely into a bowl! Use the following as a loosely-constructed guide, and don't be afraid to experiment until you figure out the right balance of flavors that works for you.

7	eggs
	Kosher salt and freshly cracked black pepper, to taste
2 1/2	cups dry salad macaroni
2	cups mayonnaise
1	tablespoon yellow mustard
1	teaspoon A.1. steak sauce
1 1/2	teaspoons Worcestershire sauce
1/2	to 3/4 cup milk
2	tablespoons sweet pickle relish
1/3	cup sweet pickle juice
4	small sweet pickles, chopped
1/4	cup finely chopped flat-leaf parsley
	Paprika, for garnish

Place the eggs in a medium saucepan and fill with enough cold water to completely submerge them. Place over high heat and bring the water to a boil. Turn off the heat and cover the saucepan with a tight-fitting lid. Let the eggs hang out for exactly 15 minutes. Drain and run cold water over them. Peel and chop 4 eggs; slice the remaining 3. Set aside.

Bring a large pot of water to a boil, generously season the water with salt. Add the macaroni and cook to al dente, according to package directions.

Meanwhile, in a medium bowl, mix together the mayonnaise, mustard, steak sauce, Worcestershire sauce, milk, pickle relish, pickle juice, and chopped pickles. The mixture may seem a bit watery, but don't panic, the pasta will absorb it like a sponge.

Drain and rinse the macaroni under cold water. Toss the wet ingredients with the pasta, along with the 4 chopped eggs and 3 tablespoons of the parsley; season with salt and pepper. Smooth the top of the salad, garnish the top with the 3 sliced eggs, the remaining parsley, and several dashes of paprika to give it that retro splash of color.

Old-Fashioned Banana Nut Bread

makes 1 loaf

Since few of us bake our own bread any-more, it has become something of a lost art. In this fast-paced world, I find it reassuring to make this kind of quick bread at home. It's also the perfect use for those overripe bananas sitting on your counter. When it's done, I love to eat thick slices toasted and sprinkled with powdered sugar.

8   tablespoons (1 stick) unsalted butter, room temperature, plus more for pan

1   cup sugar

2   large eggs

1   teaspoon pure vanilla extract

4   large ripe bananas, 3 mashed, 1 diced

2   cups all-purpose flour

1   teaspoon baking soda

1/2   teaspoon kosher salt

1   cup chopped walnuts

Preheat the oven to 350°F.

Generously butter the bottom and sides of a 9-inch loaf pan and set aside. In the bowl of a freestanding mixer fitted with a paddle attach-ment or with a handheld electric mixer, cream together the butter and sugar. With the mixer running, add the eggs one at a time, scraping down the sides of the bowl as needed. Add the vanilla and the mashed bananas, and mix until well incorporated.

In a medium bowl, whisk together the flour, baking soda, and salt. With the mixer on low, add in the dry ingredients to the wet ingredients; gently fold in the nuts and the diced banana by hand. Pour the batter into the prepared loaf pan and bake until a toothpick inserted in the center comes out clean, 55 to 60 minutes.

My Favorite Spinach Salad with Bacon serves 4

For the Dressing

1	clove garlic, minced
1/2	teaspoon lemon pepper
1/2	cup extra-virgin olive oil
2	tablespoons white vinegar

For the Salad

3	large eggs
1	pound baby spinach leaves, cleaned and drained
1/2	cup grated sharp cheddar cheese
1/2	cup cooked and crumbled bacon (about 8 slices)
1	cup good-quality croutons

Left to my own devices as a child, I would never have eaten spinach, or any other vegetable for that matter. The idea of cooked spinach is something I'm still getting used to. But raw spinach salad, fresh and bright green—that was a whole other thing. I actually used to beg for this salad. Now I serve it as a starter to a dinner party and let my guests do the begging. For more, that is.

To make the dressing, in a small bowl, whisk together the garlic, lemon pepper, oil, and vinegar. Let it hang out at room temperature for a few hours so the flavors can develop.

Place the eggs in a medium saucepan and fill with enough cold water to completely submerge them. Place over high heat and bring the water to a boil. Turn off the heat and cover the saucepan with a tight-fitting lid. Let the eggs hang out for exactly 15 minutes. Drain and run cold water over them. Peel and slice the eggs.

To make the salad, place the spinach in a large salad bowl; add the cheese and bacon. Drizzle with the salad dressing and toss lightly to coat the leaves and combine the ingredients. Garnish with the eggs and croutons.

Old-Fashioned Zucchini Bread

makes 1 loaf

On more than one occasion, my mother hornswoggled me into eating my vegetables by cleverly disguising them in things that bore a much closer resemblance to dessert. This bread became a favorite.

8 tablespoons (1 stick) unsalted butter, room temperature, plus more for pan

1 cup sugar

2 large eggs

1 teaspoon pure vanilla extract

1 3/4 cups all-purpose flour

1/2 teaspoon kosher salt

1/2 teaspoon baking soda

1/2 teaspoon freshly ground nutmeg

1/2 cup chopped walnuts

1 medium zucchini, finely grated (1 cup)

Preheat the oven to 350°F.

Generously butter the bottom and sides of a 9-inch loaf pan and set aside. In the bowl of a freestanding mixer fitted with a paddle attachment or with a handheld electric mixer, cream together the butter and sugar for several minutes until light and fluffy. Add the eggs and vanilla and mix until well incorporated.

In a medium bowl, whisk together the flour, salt, baking soda, and nutmeg. With the mixer on low, gently incorporate half of the dry ingredients into the wet, and then gently fold in the walnuts and zucchini. Finish by folding in the remainder of the dry ingredients, mixing just until the batter is moist. Pour the batter into the prepared pan. Bake until a toothpick inserted in the center comes out clean, 50 to 60 minutes.

Eggs in a Frame

serves 1

This really is more of a reminiscence than an actual recipe. It was one of the things my mom would make for me on hectic mornings before school, and one of my fondest memories.

1   slice good wheat or white sandwich bread

1   tablespoon unsalted butter

1   large egg

Kosher salt and freshly cracked black pepper

Cut a circle out of the center of the bread using a biscuit cutter or an inverted drinking glass, creating a "frame" for the egg. In a skillet over medium-high heat, heat the butter until melted and bubbling. Reduce heat to low. Place the bread "frame" in the pan and cook for 1 minute. Crack the egg into the hole, season with salt and pepper and cook until the egg is beginning to set and the bread is golden brown. Carefully flip the "frame" over with a wide spatula and finish cooking until the egg is cooked through. Serve immediately.

Just Desserts

Somebody once said, "Life is short, eat dessert first." I can't say I disagree with that philosophy. Sometimes dinner feels like just an excuse to get to the best part of the meal.

Banana Fritters with Chocolate Rum Sauce

serves 8

These fritters are ridiculously light, in spite of being battered, deep-fried, and embellished with chocolate rum sauce. Not light in calories mind you, but light in texture—not at all dense and heavy the way some fritters can be. The secret to such airiness lies in the seltzer water used to make the tempura-like batter. Two simple rules: The seltzer water must be ice-cold, and it can't be the least bit flat. If you heed that advice you will be rewarded with the most delicate, impossibly crisp fritters you've ever had. Tempted?

FOR THE SAUCE

- 8 ounces good semisweet chocolate, chopped
- 1/4 cup heavy cream
- 2 tablespoons good dark rum

FOR THE FRITTERS

- Vegetable oil, for frying
- 1/2 cup sweet rice flour, available in the Asian section of the grocery store
- 1/3 cup all-purpose flour
- 3 tablespoons sesame seeds
- 1/2 teaspoon kosher salt
- 3/4 cup ice-cold seltzer water
- 4 bananas, sliced on an angle 1/2-inch thick
- Confectioners' sugar, for dusting fritters

To make the sauce, combine the chocolate and cream in the top of a double boiler over medium-low heat (for tip, see page 163). Stir constantly until melted and smooth. Stir in the rum and remove from heat.

To make the fritters, pour 2 inches oil into a heavy-bottom frying pan or Dutch oven. Heat the oil over high heat until it registers 350°F on a deep-fry thermometer.

In a small bowl, whisk together the rice flour, all-purpose flour, sesame seeds, salt, and seltzer water until smooth and the consistency of thick pancake batter. Dip banana slices in the batter and drop gently into the hot oil. Fry until golden brown and puffy, turning once, about 2 minutes. Remove fritters to a plate lined with paper towels and dust with confectioners' sugar.

Gently reheat the chocolate rum sauce if it has gotten too thick upon cooling. Drizzle the fritters with sauce and serve immediately.

Lemon White- Chocolate Cheesecake

serves 8

This is the first cheesecake I ever had that didn't have a crust. I got over my shock after the first bite. The flavor combination is deceptively simple, yet elegant. I've never had someone try this cheesecake without begging me for the recipe. It's heaven on a plate!

5   ounces good white chocolate, chopped

2   pounds cream cheese, room temperature

1½ cups sugar

4   large eggs

    Grated zest and freshly squeezed juice of 1 lemon

1   teaspoon pure vanilla extract

Preheat the oven to 350°F.

Place a baking pan in the lower half of the oven and fill it with about 1 inch of boiling water to create a water bath.

Meanwhile, melt the white chocolate in a double boiler (for tip, see page 163), stirring frequently until smooth, or melt in the microwave for about 2 minutes on medium power. Set aside to cool slightly.

In the bowl of a freestanding mixer fitted with a paddle attachment or with a handheld electric mixer, cream together the cream cheese and sugar on medium speed until smooth. Beat in the eggs one at a time until incorporated. Scrape down the sides of the bowl with a rubber spatula and add the lemon zest and juice and the vanilla. Stir in the white chocolate and pour the filling into an ungreased 9-inch springform pan.

Bake the cheesecake in the middle of the oven, on the rack directly above the steaming water bath, until the top is light brown and the center has only a slight jiggle to it, about 1 hour.

Cool the cheesecake to room temperature, then chill in the refrigerator for at least 3 hours before serving.

Individual Chocolate Soufflés serves 4

This isn't traditional chocolate soufflé, which, believe me, even chefs find daunting. It is instead, a chocolate soufflé that is foolproof and a snap to make. Baking powder, an ingredient not found in the traditional French version, and increased amounts of flour, provide the leavening. I'm more than confident when I assure you, "It will rise."

6	ounces good bittersweet chocolate
8	tablespoons (1 stick) unsalted butter
1	cup all-purpose flour
1/2	teaspoon baking powder
1/4	teaspoon kosher salt
4	large eggs
2	teaspoons pure vanilla extract
1	cup sugar
	Confectioners' sugar, for dusting

*To make a double boiler, fill the bottom of a medium saucepan with water and place over low heat. Place chopped chocolate in a heatproof bowl on top of the saucepan. Bring the water to a gentle simmer. Do not boil. Stir frequently until chocolate is smooth and melted.

Preheat the oven to 350°F.

Place a large baking pan in the center of the oven and fill with about 1 inch boiling water to create a water bath.

Melt the chocolate and butter in a double boiler* or in the microwave for about 2 minutes on medium power. Stir until smooth and set aside to cool slightly.

Whisk the flour, baking powder, and salt together in a small bowl and set aside. Crack the eggs into the bowl of an electric mixer fitted with a whisk attachment; add the vanilla and whisk on medium speed until foamy. Add the sugar and increase speed to medium-high; whisk until the mixture thickens and lightens in color, about 2 minutes. Stir in the melted chocolate mixture and then, by hand, gently fold in the dry ingredients.

Pour the batter into four ungreased 1-cup ramekins, just shy of the top. Place the ramekins in the water bath and add more water if necessary. The water should reach no higher than a third of the way up the sides. Bake until the tops of the soufflés are slightly cracked and firm to the touch, 30 to 40 minutes. Remove the ramekins from the water bath and cool, 5 minutes. Dust with confectioners' sugar and serve warm.

Molten Chocolate Cakes with Raspberry Puree and Bananas

serves 4

FOR THE CAKES

- 6 tablespoons unsalted butter, plus more for buttering ramekins
- 1/2 cup plus 2 tablespoons sugar, plus more for sugaring ramekins
- 8 ounces good bittersweet chocolate
- 1/2 cup all-purpose flour
- 1 teaspoon kosher salt
- 4 large eggs
- 1 teaspoon pure vanilla extract
- 2 bananas, sliced on an angle, for garnish

  Fresh mint sprigs, for garnish

FOR THE RASPBERRY PUREE

- 2 cups raspberries
- 3 tablespoons water
- 2 tablespoons confectioners' sugar, or to taste

FOR THE WHIPPED CREAM

- 1 cup heavy whipping cream
- 1 teaspoon pure vanilla extract
- 2 tablespoons sugar, or to taste
- 1 large marshmallow

To make the cakes, butter 4 one-cup ramekins and sprinkle with sugar, tapping out the excess. Set aside.

Meanwhile, melt the chocolate and butter in a double boiler (for tip, see page 163) or in the microwave on medium power for about 2 minutes. Stir until smooth and set aside to cool.

Whisk together the flour, 1/2 cup sugar, and salt in a small bowl and set aside. In the bowl of a freestanding mixer fitted with a whisk attachment, beat the eggs, adding one at a time, on medium speed until the mixture is pale yellow and fluffy, about 5 minutes. Add the vanilla and whisk in the melted chocolate. Fold in the dry ingredients. Divide the batter evenly among the prepared ramekins and refrigerate, 30 minutes.

Preheat the oven to 375°F.

To make the raspberry puree, place the raspberries and water in a blender and puree until smooth. Add the confectioners' sugar, a little at a time, to taste. Place the raspberry puree in a fine-mesh sieve over a small bowl. Use a rubber spatula to force the puree through the sieve.

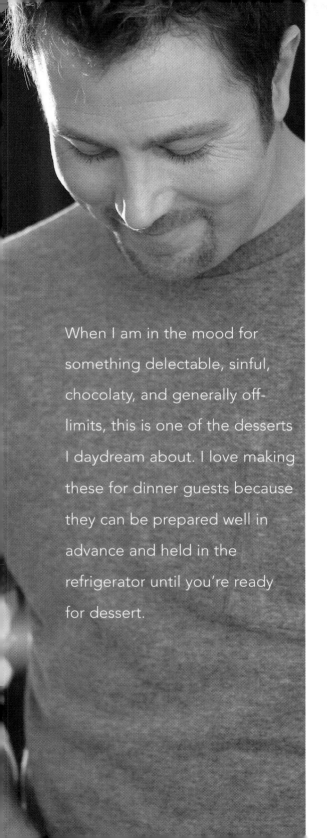

When I am in the mood for something delectable, sinful, chocolaty, and generally off-limits, this is one of the desserts I daydream about. I love making these for dinner guests because they can be prepared well in advance and held in the refrigerator until you're ready for dessert.

Remove the cakes from the refrigerator and bake until they're set on top but still have a slight jiggle in the middle. A toothpick inserted in the middle should come out with moist, not wet, batter attached, 30 to 35 minutes. Cool cakes on a rack, 10 minutes.

To make the whipped cream, use an electric mixer to whip the cream, vanilla, and sugar until soft peaks form. In a microwave oven, cook the marshmallow until soft, about ten seconds. Beat the softened marshmallow into the whipped cream, to stabilize.

To serve, run a small sharp knife around the edge of each cake and spoon raspberry puree onto 4 plates. Turn out the cakes onto the plates, dollop with whipped cream, and garnish with sliced bananas and mint sprigs.

Almond Cookies

Remember those great almond cookies you used to get at Chinese restaurants? This is my version of those delicious little cookies that once seemed so exotic to me.

makes about **20** cookies

1/4   pound raw, unpeeled almonds, plus more for garnish

2   sticks unsalted butter, room temperature

3/4   cup sugar

1   teaspoon pure vanilla extract

13/4   cups all-purpose flour

    Confectioners' sugar, for dusting

Preheat the oven to 325°F.

Line a baking sheet with parchment paper. In a food processor, grind the almonds to a fine meal.

In a freestanding electric mixer fitted with the paddle attachment or with a handheld electric mixer, cream together the butter, sugar, and the vanilla. Add the flour and ground almonds; continue mixing until well incorporated.

Divide the dough into 2 equal portions and place the mixture on a piece of parchment, arranging each portion into a log shape. Working with one roll at a time, fold the paper over the dough and pull tightly to smooth the sides of the roll. Twist the ends closed and place in the refrigerator to chill, 30 minutes. Slice into 1/4-inch rounds and press an almond into the middle of each cookie.

Arrange on the prepared pan and place in the oven to bake until lightly browned, about 10 minutes. Remove cookies to a cooling rack and wait until they have cooled slightly before dusting them with powdered sugar (otherwise the sugar will just melt right away and become sticky).

Sticky Coconut Cake

serves 12

Maybe happiness can't be bought, but it can, I believe, be baked into a cake. My idea of tropical bliss is this golden yellow cake, made extra moist by a sticky coconut glaze. The whole thing is topped with billowy clouds of whipped cream flecked with sweetened coconut.

FOR THE CAKE

1   package yellow cake mix

FOR THE GLAZE

1 1/2   cups unsweetened coconut milk

1/2   cup sugar

2   cups flaked sweetened coconut

FOR THE WHIPPED CREAM

3   cups heavy cream

1   teaspoon vanilla

1/2   cup sugar

1   large marshmallow

To make the cake, prepare the cake mix as directed on the package and bake in an ungreased 9x13-inch baking pan until a toothpick inserted in the center comes out clean.

To make the glaze, in a medium saucepan, combine the coconut milk, sugar, and 1/2 cup flaked coconut. Bring the mixture to a boil. Reduce the heat and simmer, 1 minute.

Cool the cake 10 minutes and poke the entire surface with the tines of a fork, about every inch or so. Pour the glaze evenly over the warm cake and allow it to cool completely.

To make the whipped cream, use an electric mixer to whip the cream, vanilla, and sugar until soft peaks form. In a microwave oven, cook the marshmallow until soft, about ten seconds. Beat the softened marshmallow into the whipped cream, to stabilize. Fold in 1/2 cup coconut and spread over the cake. Sprinkle the remaining 1 cup coconut over the surface of the cake. Chill the cake for several hours and store any leftovers in the refrigerator.

Chocolate Chip Cookie Dough Cheesecake

serves 8

What can I say about this one? It's cheesecake, it's cookie dough, it's divine!

FOR THE CRUST

- 2 cups graham cracker crumbs (1 package)
- 2 tablespoons sugar
- 8 tablespoons (1 stick) unsalted butter, melted

  Nonstick cooking spray

FOR THE FILLING

- 1 pound cream cheese, room temperature
- 1/2 cup sugar
- 2 large eggs
- 1 teaspoon pure vanilla extract
- 3/4 cup prepared chocolate chip cookie dough, formed into 1/2-inch blobs

Preheat the oven to 350°F.

Place a baking pan in the lower half of the oven and fill it with about 1 inch boiling water to create a water bath.

To make the crust, in a medium bowl, combine the graham cracker crumbs, sugar, and butter. Mix with a fork until moistened and well combined. Lightly coat the bottom of a 9-inch springform pan with nonstick cooking spray. Press the crumbs evenly over the bottom and up the side of the pan. Place in refrigerator to chill, 10 minutes.

Meanwhile, to make the filling, in the bowl of a freestanding mixer fitted with a paddle attachment or with a handheld electric mixer, cream together the cream cheese and sugar on medium speed until smooth. Beat in the eggs one at a time until incorporated. Scrape down the sides of the bowl with a rubber spatula and stir in the vanilla extract. Gently fold half of the cookie dough blobs into the filling. Pour into the chilled crust and dot the top with remaining blobs of cookie dough.

Bake the cheesecake in the middle of the oven, on the rack directly above the steaming water bath, until the top has light brown spots and the center has only a slight jiggle to it, 40 to 50 minutes.

Cool the cheesecake to room temperature, then chill in the refrigerator for at least 3 hours before serving.

French Apple Cobbler

For those who love apple pie, but are put off by the idea of making and rolling out pie pastry, this simple cobbler recipe is for you. You get all the flavor of tart apples and cinnamon, plus an unexpected hint of vanilla, with a fraction of the work. A definite winner in my book!

FOR THE FILLING

5	cups peeled and thinly sliced Granny Smith apples
3/4	cup sugar
2	tablespoons all-purpose flour
1/2	teaspoon cinnamon
	Pinch of kosher salt
1	teaspoon pure vanilla extract
1	tablespoon unsalted butter, room temperature

FOR THE TOPPING

1	cup all-purpose flour
1	cup sugar
1	teaspoon baking powder
1/2	teaspoon kosher salt
4	tablespoons (1/2 stick) unsalted butter, melted
1	large egg, slightly beaten

Preheat the oven to 350°F

To make the filling, combine the sliced apples, sugar, flour, cinnamon, salt, and vanilla in a large bowl and mix to combine. Pour the filling into an ungreased 9x13-inch baking dish and dot with softened butter.

To make the topping, whisk together the flour, sugar, baking powder, and salt in a medium bowl. Stir in the melted butter and egg until the batter is smooth and well combined. Drop large spoonfuls of the batter randomly over the apples; the batter will not completely cover the filling, but will expand during baking.

Bake until bubbling and golden brown, 35 to 40 minutes. Serve with fresh whipped cream or vanilla ice cream.

Flourless Chocolate Cake with Orange-Scented Whipped Cream

serves 8 to 10

FOR THE CAKE

12 ounces good bittersweet chocolate

12 tablespoons unsalted butter

6   eggs, separated

12 tablespoons sugar

1   tablespoon pure vanilla extract

FOR THE WHIPPED CREAM

1   cup heavy whipping cream

1   teaspoon pure vanilla extract

2   tablespoons sugar, or to taste

1   large marshmallow

Grated zest of 1 orange

Preheat the oven to 350°F.

Line the bottom of a 9-inch springform pan with parchment paper and set aside. To make the cake, melt the chocolate and butter in a double boiler (for tip, see page 163) or in the microwave for about 2 minutes on medium power. Stir until smooth and set aside to cool.

In a medium bowl, use an electric mixer to beat the egg yolks with 6 tablespoons of the sugar until the mixture is pale yellow and fluffy, about 5 minutes. Add the vanilla and fold in the melted chocolate. Set aside.

Beat the egg whites using a freestanding or handheld electric mixer until soft peaks form. Gradually add the remaining 6 tablespoons sugar and beat until medium-firm, but not dry, peaks form. Lighten the chocolate mixture by folding in one-third of the egg whites gently into the chocolate mixture, then fold in the remainder, being careful to just incorporate; don't overwork the batter—a few white streaks

This cake is something between a soufflé and a dense chocolate brownie. And somewhere (in my estimation) between nirvana and heaven. If indeed there is such a place. If there is, and if I make it there, I want to eat this cake every single day.

are okay. Pour into prepared pan and bake in the center of the oven until the top is puffed and cracked and a tester inserted in the middle comes out with moist crumbs attached, 40 to 50 minutes. Cool completely on a wire rack. Don't be alarmed when the center sinks in and forms a crater. To release, run a small sharp knife around the edge of the cake and release the sides of the pan.

To make the orange-scented whipped cream, use an electric mixer to whip the cream, vanilla, and sugar until soft peaks form. In a microwave oven, cook the marshmallow until soft, about 10 seconds. Add the orange zest to the whipped cream and beat in the softened marshmallow, to stabilize. Dollop the cream in the center of the cake and serve in large slices. Pure chocolate bliss!

Neiman Marcus Chocolate Chip Cookies

You've probably heard the urban legend about the woman who was so enraptured with the chocolate chip cookies at Neiman Marcus that she asked for the recipe. She was told it would cost "two-fifty." She agreed and had them charge it to her account. To her horror, when the bill arrived it was for $250! Outraged, she decided to get even. She quickly dispersed the recipe to every one she knew and asked them to do the same. It turns out that the story isn't at all true. Not even a little bit. But urban legend or not, this is truly the best chocolate chip cookie I have ever tasted.

makes about 4 dozen cookies

1	pound (4 sticks) unsalted butter, room temperature
2	cups granulated sugar
2	cups packed light brown sugar
4	large eggs
2	teaspoons pure vanilla extract
5	cups oatmeal
4	cups all-purpose flour
1	teaspoon kosher salt
2	teaspoons baking powder
2	teaspoons baking soda
24	ounces semisweet chocolate chips
1	regular-size Hershey bar, grated
3	cups chopped walnuts

Preheat the oven to 375°F.

Line a baking sheet with parchment paper. In a freestanding electric mixer fitted with a paddle attachment or with a handheld electric mixer, cream together the butter and both sugars. Add the eggs and vanilla; mix well to incorporate. Place the oatmeal in a blender and grind to a fine powder. Whisk the oatmeal, flour, salt, baking powder, and baking soda together in a medium bowl. Stir into the wet ingredients. Mix on low speed to form the dough. Fold in the chocolate chips, grated chocolate, and walnuts using a wooden spoon or rubber spatula, so as not to break them up or melt the chocolate with the heat of the mixer.

Roll the dough into golf ball-size rounds and place 2 inches apart on the prepared pan. Bake until the tops of the cookies crack and turn golden brown, 10 to 14 minutes. (The key is to slightly underbake them so the cookie stays soft and chewy.) Remove the cookies to a rack and cool completely. Store in an airtight container.

Banana (Chimpanzee) Cheesecake serves 8

I run the risk of offending true cheesecake purists here, but I simply cannot resist. The best I can hope for is to bring you over to my side, the side of creamy banana-spiked cheesecake on top of a crumbly graham cracker crust. Trust me on this one.

FOR THE CRUST

- 2 cups graham cracker crumbs (1 package)
- 2 tablespoons sugar
- 8 tablespoons (1 stick) unsalted butter, melted
- Nonstick cooking spray

FOR THE FILLING

- 1 pound cream cheese, room temperature
- 3/4 cup sugar
- 4 large eggs
- 1 teaspoon pure vanilla extract
- 2 teaspoons freshly squeezed lemon juice
- 1 cup sour cream
- 1 cup ripe bananas, mashed (about 3 medium bananas)

Preheat the oven to 350°F.

Place a baking pan in the lower half of the oven and fill it with about 1 inch boiling water to create a water bath.

To make the crust, in a medium bowl, combine the graham cracker crumbs, sugar, and butter. Mix with a fork until moistened and well combined. Lightly coat the bottom of a 9-inch springform pan with nonstick cooking spray. Press the crumbs evenly over the bottom and up the side of the pan. Place in refrigerator for 10 minutes, while you get on with the filling.

To make the filling, in the bowl of a freestanding mixer fitted with a paddle attachment or with a handheld electric mixer on medium speed, cream together the cream cheese and sugar until smooth. Beat in the eggs one at a time until incorporated. Scrape down the sides of the bowl with a rubber spatula and add the vanilla and lemon juice. Fold in the sour cream and mashed bananas. Pour the filling into the crust.

Bake the cheesecake in the middle of the oven, on the rack directly above the steaming water bath, until the top is light brown and the center has a slight jiggle to it, about 1 hour. Turn off the oven and cool the cheesecake in the oven to room temperature. Chill in the refrigerator for at least 3 hours before serving.

Baked Alaska Lemons

serves 8

This is an entirely manageable version of Baked Alaska, that high-maintenance retro dish from my mother's era. So named, I imagine, for its icy cold interior. Here, the use of sorbet (instead of the traditional ice cream) lessens the guilt factor. That, coupled with the fact that these are individually sized, well, it's everything you could possibly ask for in a dessert. Sweetness and light.

8	small lemons
1	pint lemon sorbet, slightly softened
3	egg whites, room temperature
1/8	teaspoon cream of tartar
2/3	cup sugar

Slice one end off of each lemon to make a flat base Cut 1/3 off of the other end. Using a small paring knife and a grapefruit spoon, scoop out the flesh of the lemon, much like you would the inside of a pumpkin, to make a clean shell. Fill each lemon shell with the softened sorbet. Level off the top and freeze until solid, about 2 hours.

Just before serving, place the egg whites and cream of tartar in the bowl of a freestanding mixer fitted with a whisk attachment. Whip on medium-high speed until foamy. Slowly add the sugar and continue to whip until stiff, but not dry, peaks form, about 3 minutes total. Spoon the meringue into a pastry bag fitted with a star tip and top the sorbet with the meringue, making sure to seal the edges. You can also spoon the meringue on top of the lemons.

Use a propane torch to brown the meringue, or place the lemons under a broiler with the rack about 7 inches away from the heat, turning as needed, until golden brown. The lemons can be served immediately or placed in the freezer until needed. Just make sure to remove them about 20 minutes before you plan to serve them. You want them to be frozen, but not rock hard.

Chocolate Decadence with Raspberry Puree

serves 8

FOR THE CAKE

Nonstick cooking spray

5   ounces good bittersweet chocolate, chopped

1   large egg

1   egg yolk

1   teaspoon pure vanilla extract

2   egg whites

1/8   teaspoon cream of tartar

1/2   cup plus 1/2 tablespoon cocoa powder

2   tablespoons all-purpose flour

2/3   cup plus 1/4 cup sugar

3/4   cup whole milk

Homemade whipped cream, for garnish

Mint sprigs, for garnish

FOR THE RASPBERRY PUREE

2   cups fresh raspberries, plus a few more for garnish

3   tablespoons water

2   tablespoons confectioners' sugar, or to taste

Preheat the oven to 350°F.

Place a large baking pan in the lower third of the oven of the oven and fill with about 1 inch boiling water to create a water bath. Spray the sides of an 8-inch round cake pan with nonstick cooking spray and line the bottom with parchment paper.

Place the chocolate in a large bowl. In a small bowl, mix one whole egg and one egg yolk with the vanilla extract. Place the egg whites in the bowl of a freestanding mixer with the cream of tartar and set all three bowls aside.

Combine the cocoa, flour, and 2/3 cup sugar in a medium saucepan. Whisk in enough milk to make a paste. Whisk in the remaining milk and cook over medium heat until simmering. Simmer gently, 1 1/2 minutes. Pour the hot mixture over the chopped chocolate and mix until smooth. Whisk the egg and vanilla mixture into the chocolate and set aside.

While this recipe is by no means difficult, it is a bit involved. Don't let that scare you. I cannot encourage you enough to try it. Chocolate Decadence is habit-forming and the finished result is incredibly delicious.

Beat the egg whites and cream of tartar on medium speed until soft peaks form. Gradually sprinkle in the remaining 1/4 cup sugar; increase the mixer speed to high and beat until stiff, but not dry. Fold a quarter of the egg whites into the chocolate, to lighten. Gently fold in the remaining egg whites and pour the batter into the prepared cake pan. Set the cake pan in the hot water bath. Bake exactly 30 minutes.

Cool the finished cake completely on a cooling rack and chill 8 hours or overnight. Unmold by sliding a knife around the edge of the cake before inverting onto a serving plate.

To make the raspberry puree, place the raspberries and water in a blender and puree until smooth. Add the confectioners' sugar, a little at a time, to taste. Place the puree in a fine-mesh sieve set over a small bowl. Use a rubber spatula to force the puree through the sieve.

To serve, dip a large knife in hot water and slice the cake carefully; wipe the knife clean between each cut. Puddle the raspberry puree in the middle of each plate and set a piece of the cake in the center of the puddle. Top with a dollop of whipped cream and garnish with a few raspberries and a sprig of mint.

Strawberries in Port

serves 2

There is something so sophisticated and—dare I say it?—sexy about strawberries and port wine served in a champagne glass. It's just the kind of dessert you can serve as a finale to a romantic dinner. A sip of champagne complements the berries perfectly and really takes them over the top.

1   cup good port wine

1/2   cup sugar

1/4   teaspoon pure vanilla extract

1   cup fresh strawberries, hulled

10   fresh mint leaves, chopped

In a medium saucepan over medium-high heat, combine the wine and sugar. Bring to a boil and simmer gently until reduced by a third, 10 to 15 minutes. Remove from the heat and stir in the vanilla. Cool to room temperature and toss with the strawberries and chopped mint. Cover and allow the berries to macerate for several hours at room temperature. Serve in champagne glasses.

Lavender Crème Brûlée

serves 6

People think of crème brûlée as something you order in a fancy restaurant, not something you make at home. In fact, it is ridiculously easy to make, and perfuming the custard with dried lavender flowers really makes it something special.

Nonstick cooking spray

4   cups heavy cream

1   tablespoon dried lavender flowers*

8   large egg yolks

3/4   cup sugar

Dried lavender flowers can be found in gourmet kitchen stores or ordered online.

Preheat the oven to 300°F.

Place a large baking dish in the center of the oven and fill it with about 1 inch of boiling water to create a water bath.

Meanwhile, spray 6 half-cup crème brûlée ramekins with nonstick cooking spray. Pour the cream into a large, heavy saucepan over medium heat; add the lavender. Scald the cream by bringing it almost to a boil. Remove from heat and allow to steep, 5 minutes. Strain through a fine-mesh sieve to remove the lavender flowers.

In a large bowl, whisk together the egg yolks and half of the sugar until light and creamy. Slowly add the cream to the egg mixture, a little at a time, whisking constantly. You want to temper, not scramble the eggs.

Pour the custard into the ramekins, filling them almost to the top. Place the ramekins in the hot water bath and add more water if necessary to bring it half way up the sides.

Bake until the custard is set around the edges but still has a slight jiggle in the middle, about 40 to 45 minutes. Begin checking at 30 minutes. Remove from the oven and let the custards cool in the water bath for 30 minutes, then chill for at least 2 hours.

When ready to serve, sprinkle the remaining sugar over the custards and, using a small handheld torch, caramelize the tops until they bubble and turn golden brown. If you don't have a torch, place the ramekins on a sheet pan 6 inches below the broiler for a few minutes to achieve the same effect. Refrigerate for 10 minutes before serving.

Black-Bottom Cupcakes

makes 12 cupcakes

I'd all but forgotten about these little chocolate gems with their tender cream cheese bellies, until my mom reminded me of how much I used to love them. I would beg for these whenever there was a bake sale at school. In fact, I once told my mom there was a bake sale just to get her to make them for me.

FOR THE CUPCAKES

2 1/4   cups all-purpose flour

1 1/2   cups sugar

1 1/2   teaspoons baking soda

3/4   teaspoon kosher salt

1/4   cup plus 2 tablespoons cocoa powder

1 1/2   cups water

1/3   cup plus 3 tablespoons vegetable oil

1 1/2   teaspoons white vinegar

1 1/2   teaspoons pure vanilla extract

FOR THE FILLING

1/4   pound cream cheese, room temperature

1/2   cup sugar

1/8   teaspoon kosher salt

1   large egg

6   ounces semisweet chocolate chips

Preheat the oven to 350°F.

Line 12 muffin cups with paper liners. To make the cake batter, in a medium bowl, whisk together the flour, sugar, baking soda, salt, and cocoa. Add the water, oil, vinegar, and vanilla and stir together until smooth and well combined.

To make the filling, in the bowl of a freestanding mixer fitted with a paddle attachment or with a handheld electric mixer, cream together the cream cheese, suger, and salt. Add the egg and mix until well incorporated. Gently fold in the chocolate chips by hand.

Fill the muffin cups 2/3 full with the cake batter and drop a tablespoon-size dollop of the cream cheese filling in the middle.

Bake until the tops are firm and a toothpick inserted in the cupcakes comes out clean, 25 to 30 minutes.

Blueberry Scones

makes 8 scones

These scones capitalize on the "made-for-each-other" combination of blueberry and lemon and require (in my opinion) no further embellishment of butter, Devonshire cream, or jam. They're nothing like the heavy, dry, and crumbly scones that may have turned you off in the past. The secret to their dreamy lightness lies in taking extreme care not to overwork the dough. I feel confident proclaiming these to be the best scones I've ever tasted, a sentiment echoed by everyone who has ever tasted these still warm from the oven.

2	cups all-purpose flour, plus more for dusting
5	teaspoons granulated sugar
1	tablespoon baking powder
1/2	teaspoon kosher salt
	Grated zest of 2 lemons
9	tablespoons very cold unsalted butter, diced
1 1/2	cups fresh blueberries
1/3	cup heavy cream, plus more for brushing tops
2	large eggs
	Raw turbinado sugar, for sprinkling tops

Preheat the oven to 400°F.

Line a sheet pan with parchment paper. In a large bowl whisk together the flour, sugar, baking powder, salt, and lemon zest. Add the butter and work it into the flour mixture with a pastry cutter or by pressing it between your fingers until the mixture resembles coarse meal and the butter is about the size of peas. Using your fingers, gently toss the blueberries with the flour mixture. At this point, place the bowl in the refrigerator to keep the butter cold.

In a medium bowl, whisk together 1/3 cup cream and the eggs. Take the flour mixture out of the refrigerator and make a well in the center; pour in the eggs and cream. Using the tines of a fork and working from the outside of the flour mixture, gently start incorporating the dry ingredients into the wet until just combined, being careful not to mash the berries. The key is not to overwork the dough, but to just bring it together. It will be crumbly, but that's exactly what makes a moist, tender scone in the end.

Lightly dust your work surface with flour and turn the dough out onto it. Gently knead the dough and pat it out into a 6-inch square. Using a knife or a pastry bench scraper, cut the dough into 4 equal squares. Cut each square in half on the diagonal to make 8 triangles. Carefully transfer the scones to the prepared sheet pans. Brush the tops with cream and sprinkle with raw sugar. Bake until lightly golden brown, about 18 to 20 minutes. Cool slightly on a wire rack and serve warm.

Variation:
To make Cinnamon Chocolate Scones, substitute 2 teaspoons ground cinnamon for the lemon zest and 1 1/2 cups chopped bittersweet chocolate chunks for the fresh blueberries.

Old-Fashioned Banana Cream Pie

serves 8

FOR THE CRUST

1 1/4   cups all-purpose flour

1/2   teaspoon kosher salt

1/2   teaspoon sugar

8   tablespoons (1 stick) very cold unsalted butter, cut into pieces

2   to 4 tablespoons ice water

FOR THE FILLING

3   egg yolks

1/3   cup all-purpose flour

3/4   cup sugar

1/4   teaspoon kosher salt

2   cups whole milk

2   tablespoons unsalted butter, cut into pieces

1   teaspoon pure vanilla extract

1   teaspoon banana extract

2   ripe bananas

1   tablespoon freshly squeezed lemon juice

FOR THE WHIPPED CREAM

1 1/2   cups heavy cream

1   teaspoon pure vanilla extract

3   to 4 tablespoons sugar, or to taste

1   large marshmallow

To make the crust, place the flour, salt, and sugar in the bowl of a food processor; add the butter pieces and pulse several times to combine until the mixture resembles peas. Slowly add the ice water through the feed tube and mix just until the dough comes together. Turn the dough out onto a lightly floured board and press into a flat disk. Wrap the dough in plastic wrap and place in the refrigerator to chill, 1 hour.

To make the filling, lightly beat the egg yolks in a medium bowl and set aside. Mix together the flour, sugar, and salt and place in a medium saucepan. Over medium heat, whisk in the milk, stirring constantly until mixture comes to a boil. Cook for 2 minutes and remove from heat. Ladle a small amount of the hot milk mixture into the yolks, whisking constantly, to temper*. Add the yolks to the saucepan and stir constantly, 2 minutes. Remove from heat and whisk in the butter, vanilla, and banana extract. Strain the custard through a fine-mesh sieve into a medium bowl and place in the refrigerator to chill, about 2 hours.

Preheat the oven to 375°F.

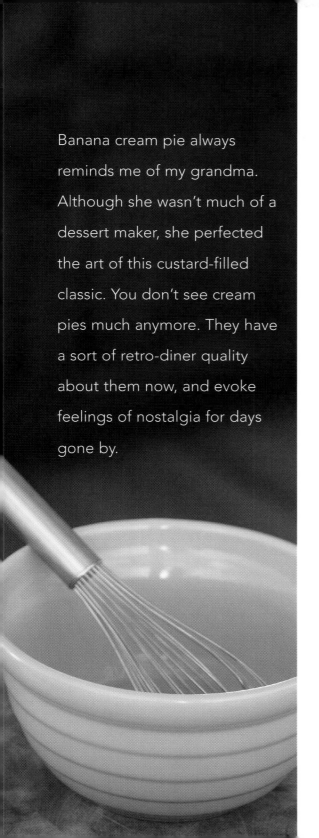

Banana cream pie always reminds me of my grandma. Although she wasn't much of a dessert maker, she perfected the art of this custard-filled classic. You don't see cream pies much anymore. They have a sort of retro-diner quality about them now, and evoke feelings of nostalgia for days gone by.

Roll the dough into a circle about 1/8 inch thick. Gently roll the dough over itself onto a rolling pin and place in the pie plate, pressing it into the sides. Trim the edges, leaving a 1-inch overhang. Fold under and flute. Carefully line the pie shell edges with aluminum foil to prevent over-browning; be careful not to damage the dough. Fill with pie weights or dried beans and bake until golden brown, 15 to 18 minutes. Let cool completely.

To make the whipped cream, use a freestanding or handheld electric mixer to whip the cream, vanilla, and sugar until soft peaks form. In a microwave oven, cook the marshmallow until soft, about ten seconds. Stir the marshmallow into the whipped cream, to stabilize.

Slice the bananas 1/4 inch thick and toss with the lemon juice. Line the bottom of the pie shell with the bananas and pour the cooled custard over them. Garnish the top of the pie with whipped cream. Refrigerate for several hours and serve well chilled.

*Tempering is the technique used to blend uncooked eggs into hot liquid or sauce. Eggs are beaten and a little of the hot mixture is stirred into them to warm (temper) them. Tempering slowly raises the temperature of an egg without curdling it.

Watergate Pie

serves 8

FOR THE CRUST

- 1   cup walnuts
- 8   tablespoons (1 stick) unsalted butter, room temperature
- 1   cup all-purpose flour

FOR THE FIRST FILLING

- 1 1/2   cups heavy cream
- 2   teaspoons pure vanilla extract
- 1   large marshmallow
- 1/2   pound cream cheese, room temperature
- 1   cup confectioners' sugar, sifted
- 2   to 3 tablespoons sugar, or to taste

FOR THE SECOND FILLING

- 2   (3-ounce) packages instant pistachio pudding mix
- 2 1/2   cups milk
- 2   tablespoons slivered unsalted pistachios, for garnish

Theories abound on the origin of this kitschy psychedelic green dessert. It was a '70s specialty of my aunt Mona and a childhood favorite of mine. According to culinary folk-lore, Kraft Foods developed a recipe for Pistachio Pineapple Delight in 1976 to launch their newest instant pudding flavor, pistachio. A *Chicago Tribune* food editor reprinted the recipe, renaming it Watergate Salad to generate reader interest. Other recipe creations cashed in on the scandal of the day, including Watergate Cake with Cover-Up Frosting and my favorite, Watergate Pie.

My aunt used (as was popular in the day) whipped topping from a tub. I've updated the recipe with fresh whipped cream and a garnish of slivered pistachios.

Preheat the oven to 350°F.

To make the crust, add the walnuts to the bowl of a food processor and pulse several times to chop finely. Add the butter and flour; process to combine and form a dough. Press into a deep-dish pie plate. Bake until the crust is golden brown, 25 to 20 minutes. Set aside to cool completely.

Meanwhile, to make the first filling, use a free-standing or handheld electric mixer to whip the cream and vanilla until soft peaks form. In a microwave oven, cook the marshmallow until soft, about 10 seconds. Beat the softened marshmallow into the whipped cream, to stabilize.

Using an electric mixer, mix together 1 cup of the whipped cream, the softened cream cheese, and the confectioners' sugar. Spread the mixture over the bottom of the crust. Mix the remaining whipped cream with the granulated sugar and set aside.

To make the second filling, in a medium bowl, whisk together the pudding mix and the milk until smooth and thickened, 3 to 4 minutes. Pour the pudding over the cream cheese layer. Top with the remaining whipped cream and sprinkle with slivered pistachios. Refrigerate for several hours and serve chilled.

Mixology

A great cocktail needs no introduction. Whether you like them shaken or stirred, if you're throwing a swanky ultra-lounge party, or you just need a stiff drink after a hard day, you're sure to find something to suit your fancy in the following pages. It's not hard to see that frou-frou drinks have a fond place in my heart. After you sample a few of them, they will have a fond place in your heart as well. Cheers!

Sparkling Shiraz from Down Under

I have a secret I'm dying to let you in on. Are you ready? Lean closer… It's sparkling Shiraz. Or "spurgles" as the Aussies fondly refer to it.

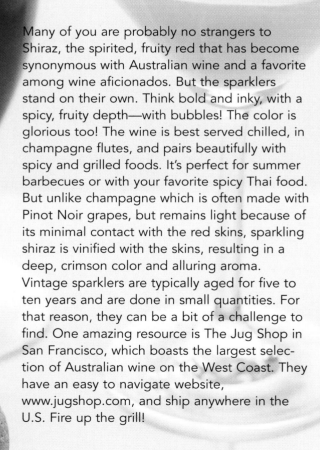

Many of you are probably no strangers to Shiraz, the spirited, fruity red that has become synonymous with Australian wine and a favorite among wine aficionados. But the sparklers stand on their own. Think bold and inky, with a spicy, fruity depth—with bubbles! The color is glorious too! The wine is best served chilled, in champagne flutes, and pairs beautifully with spicy and grilled foods. It's perfect for summer barbecues or with your favorite spicy Thai food. But unlike champagne which is often made with Pinot Noir grapes, but remains light because of its minimal contact with the red skins, sparkling shiraz is vinified with the skins, resulting in a deep, crimson color and alluring aroma. Vintage sparklers are typically aged for five to ten years and are done in small quantities. For that reason, they can be a bit of a challenge to find. One amazing resource is The Jug Shop in San Francisco, which boasts the largest selection of Australian wine on the West Coast. They have an easy to navigate website, www.jugshop.com, and ship anywhere in the U.S. Fire up the grill!

Green Apple Martini

serves 1

Okay, the Green Apple Martini may seem a bit passé. Maybe it is, but this drink, along with the Cosmopolitan, is still one of the most requested cocktails at any party I have hosted or catered. Maybe it's because it just looks like a party! It's Day-Glo green, has a sense of humor, and tastes like a Jolly Rancher! I've included a couple of variations in case you want to take things a step further.

3 ounces vodka

3 ounces Apple Pucker

1 1/2 ounces sweet-and-sour mix

1 1/2 ounces 7-Up

1 thin slice green apple, for garnish

Pour the vodka, Apple Pucker, sweet-and-sour, and 7-Up into a cocktail shaker. Tumble in a handful of ice and shake vigorously. Strain into a chilled martini glass and float a thin slice of green apple on the top.

Variations:
Caramel Apple Martini: Add 1 1/2 ounces caramel-flavored syrup to the mix before shaking.

For a little extra color, add a splash of grenadine after straining into the glass, but don't stir! Otherwise, you'll just end up with a mottled mess. The syrup will settle to the bottom and add an extra layer of color and flavor. Garnish with a maraschino cherry.

Chocolate Martini serves 1

1 ounce good dark chocolate, melted, for garnish

3 ounces vanilla vodka

3 ounces Godiva chocolate liqueur

2 ounces Crème de Cacao

Splash of half-and-half

I've tried many versions of this drink. Some are transparent and some, like this one, are more milky-looking. They're all good, but this one happens to be my favorite. The Chocolate Martini is extremely rich—a dessert in itself.

Dip the rim of a martini glass in the melted chocolate and place in the freezer for several minutes to allow the chocolate to harden. Meanwhile, pour the vodka, Godiva liqueur, Crème de Cacao, and half-and-half into a cocktail shaker. Tumble in a handful of ice and shake vigorously. Strain into the chilled, chocolate-rimmed glass. Cheers!

The French Martini serves 1

2 ounces vodka

1 ounce Chambord (raspberry liqueur)

4 ounces pineapple juice

Although an authentic French Martini is a before-dinner drink made with Lillet, this is what most Americans have come to know as the French Martini. I was first introduced to this drink by a girlfriend who insists it's the next big thing.

Pour the vodka, Chambord, and pineapple juice into a cocktail shaker. Tumble in a handful of ice and shake vigorously. Strain into a chilled martini glass.

Cosmopolitan serves 1

3 ounces vodka

3 ounces cranberry juice

1 1/2 ounces Rose's Lime Juice

1 1/2 ounces Triple Sec

Twist of lime, for garnish

The Cosmopolitan, or "Cosmo" as the cool people call it, has gained much popularity over the last few years. Once considered a "girly drink," it's not uncommon to find men sidling up to the bar and ordering it. However, they always seem to ask for a different glass. I use Rose's Sweetened Lime Juice in this recipe. If you prefer your drink less sweet and more tart, feel free to use the same amount of fresh-squeezed.

Pour the vodka, cranberry juice, lime juice, and Triple Sec into a cocktail shaker. Tumble in a handful of ice and shake vigorously. Strain into a chilled martini glass; garnish with a twist of lime.

Creamsicle® Martini

serves 1

I used to chase down the ice cream man for this flavor combination. Now, of course, I'm much more partial to the spiked version in a martini glass.

1 1/2 ounces vanilla vodka

1 ounce mandarin-flavored vodka

1 ounce freshly squeezed orange juice

1 ounce fresh pineapple juice

1 ounce Triple Sec

Splash of half-and-half

Pour the vodkas, orange juice, pineapple juice, Triple Sec, and half-and-half into a cocktail shaker. Tumble in a handful of ice and shake vigorously. Strain into a chilled martini glass.

Banana-Nut Martini serves 1

When I first moved to Los Angeles, a good friend convinced me to go on a blind date. Against my better judgment, I agreed. We met at a tapas bar, and although I don't remember the name of the bar or the name of my date, I do remember this drink. I did my best to re-create it at home.

Pour the vodka, banana liqueur, and a splash of Frangelico into a cocktail shaker. Tumble in a handful of ice and shake vigorously. Strain into a chilled martini glass and float a banana slice on top.

Go lightly with the Frangelico. The flavor is intense and has a tendency to overpower the drink. You just want a hint of the flavor in the background.

3   ounces vodka

3   ounces banana liqueur

     Splash of Frangelico liqueur*

1   banana, sliced, for garnish

Key Lime Pie Martini serves 1

     Lime wedge

     Finely crushed graham crackers, for garnish

4   ounces vanilla vodka

1   ounce Rose's Sweetened Lime Juice

1   ounce pineapple juice

1   ounce Midori

     Splash of half-and-half

Some things just make perfect sense. Like driving around South Beach listening to Will Smith's "Miami" blasting on the car stereo (cheesy, I know!), and drinking Key Lime Pie Martinis late into the night.

Run a lime wedge along the rim of a chilled martini glass and dip the rim in the graham cracker crumbs. Pour the vodka, lime juice, pineapple juice, Midori, and half-and-half into a cocktail shaker. Tumble in a handful of ice and shake vigorously. Strain into the martini glass. Dessert in cocktail form!

S'Moretini serves 1

The word "s'mores," always used in the plural, is short for "some more," referring to one's appetite for more than just one. You'll get the same request for this drink.

Finely crushed graham crackers, for garnish

Chocolate syrup

1 1/2 ounces vanilla vodka

1 ounce white Godiva liqueur

1 ounce dark Godiva liqueur

Mini marshmallows, for garnish

Wet the rim of a chilled martini glass with water and dip in the graham cracker crumbs. Drizzle chocolate syrup around the inside of the glass. Pour the vodka and Godiva liqueurs into a cocktail shaker. Tumble in a handful of ice and shake vigorously. Strain into a chilled martini glass and float a few marshmallows on top. The only thing that's missing is the campfire.

Fresh Watermelon Martini serves 1

3 ounces fresh seedless watermelon (about three 1-inch cubes)

3 ounces vodka

1 1/2 ounces sweet-and-sour mix

1 1/2 ounces freshly squeezed lime juice

Sugar, to taste (optional)

Thanks to a certain show on HBO, it seems we all went through a fixation with a little drink called the Cosmopolitan—at least I did. This is a slight variation on that theme. It uses fresh watermelon and really is the perfect summer drink.

Cut the watermelon into chunks and purée in a blender until smooth. Pour the watermelon puree, vodka, sweet-and-sour, lime juice, and sugar, if using, into a cocktail shaker. Tumble in a handful of ice and shake vigorously. Strain into a chilled martini glass. Summer has officially arrived!

Pomegranate Margaritas

serves 4

Most of us are familiar with strawberry, mango, and even raspberry versions of the classic margarita. But isn't it true that familiarity breeds contempt? That reason alone inspired me to shake things up a bit and find a new spin on this old favorite.

1   cup pure pomegranate juice

2   tablespoons freshly squeezed lime juice

1   cup Triple Sec

1   cup white tequila

3   cups ice

     Lime wedges, for garnish

Combine the pomegranate juice, lime juice, Triple Sec, tequila, and ice in a blender and pulverize until completely blended. Serve in frozen martini glasses and garnish with lime wedges.

Watermelon Margaritas

serves 2

There's a great little restaurant in New York's Chelsea neighborhood called Food Bar. On the recommendation of our spunky Jennifer Jason Leigh look-a-like waitress I decided to give their watermelon margaritas a try. The food was great, but the margaritas were heavenly. Perhaps it's no coincidence that they served them on the rocks in a tall glass that once held a 7-day religious Veladora candle.

12   ounces fresh seedless watermelon (about twelve 1-inch cubes)

$1/2$ cup white tequila

$1/2$ cup Triple Sec

$1/2$ cup sweet-and-sour mix

     Freshly squeezed juice of $1/2$ lime

Cut the watermelon into chunks and purée in a blender until smooth. Pour the watermelon puree, tequila, Triple Sec, sweet-and-sour, and lime juice into a pitcher and stir. Pour over ice in large glasses and serve.

Tequila-Fruit Infusion

serves a party

There is no wrong answer here—add whatever combination of fruits you like or happen to have on hand. The tequila will take on whatever flavors you add to it. I like to make this in a large jar with a spigot and eat the drunken fruit while sipping the tequila slowly. This stuff tastes like candy and goes down very easy—it really sneaks up on you. Consider yourself warned.

For purely aesthetic purposes, layer the fruit artfully in the bottom of a large jar or pitcher and pour the tequila over it. Let it steep overnight at room temperature; the fruit will dye the tequila a beautiful pinkish color and take the bite out of the alcohol. Shake over ice and serve in chilled martini glasses.

- 4 white peaches, pitted and sliced
- 4 kiwis, peeled and sliced
- 1 fresh pineapple, cored and sliced
- 2 pints strawberries, hulled and sliced
- 2 (750ml) bottles silver tequila

German Chocolate Cake Martini

serves 1

If it were possible to pour a slice of German chocolate cake into a chilled martini glass, and sip headily, this is what it would taste like. Have your cake and drink it, too!

- 1 1/2 ounces vanilla vodka
- 3 ounces Godiva chocolate liqueur
- 2 ounces Malibu coconut rum
- 1 1/2 ounces Coco Lopez sweetened coconut milk

Splash of Kahlúa liqueur

Pour the vodka, Godiva liqueur, coconut rum, Coco Lopez, and Kahlúa into a cocktail shaker. Tumble in a handful of ice and shake vigorously. Strain into a chilled martini glass.

Cuban Mojito serves 1

Even though I love this drink, I always found making it a bit labor intensive with all that stirring and muddling and waiting for the sugar to melt. That is, until a friend told me to try confectioners' sugar, because it melts faster. It was an inspired moment and I've never looked back.

Squeeze the juice from the lime halves into a tall glass. Cut each lime half into quarters and toss them into the glass. Add the confectioners' sugar and the mint leaves and muddle* the whole thing together with the handle of a wooden spoon. Tumble in a handful of ice and pour in the rum. Add club soda to fill the glass, give it a good stir, and garnish with a lime wedge.

Muddling means to mash everything together in the bottom of the glass. It releases the juice of the limes and the essential oils of the mint leaves.

1   lime, halved

3   tablespoons confectioners' sugar, or to taste

12 fresh mint leaves

3   ounces white rum

    Club soda

    Lime wedge, for garnish

Limeade Vodka serves 1
Cocktail

3   ounces vodka

2   ounces limeade concentrate

    Club soda

    Lime wedge, for garnish

I came up with this one night when unexpected guests dropped in and all I had on hand was a bottle of well-chilled vodka and some limeade concentrate. This is what I call a happy accident.

Stir the vodka and limeade concentrate together in a tall glass. Tumble in a handful of ice, top off with the club soda, and stir. Garnish with a lime wedge.

Pomegranate Mojito

serves 1

This drink draws inspiration from the classic Cuban Mojito, but bends tradition with the addition of pomegranate.

1/2   lime

1   tablespoon raw turbinado sugar, or to taste

12   fresh mint leaves

6   tablespoons white rum

1/4   cup pure pomegranate juice

    Club soda

    Lime wedge, for garnish

Squeeze the juice from the lime half into a small glass, then cut the lime half into quarters and toss them into the glass. Add the raw sugar and the mint leaves and muddle* the whole thing together with the handle of a wooden spoon. Tumble in a handful of ice and pour in the rum. Add the pomegranate juice, give it a good stir, and top it off with a bit of club soda. Garnish with a lime wedge. Hello cocktail hour!

Muddling means to mash everything together in the bottom of the glass. It releases the juice of the limes and the essential oils of the mint leaves.

Spiced Orange Latte

serves 2

This makes for a nice alternative to the traditional caffeine-laden espresso drink and is just the thing when you're in the mood for something sweet. Children love this drink, too.

2   cups milk

1/4   cup packed light brown sugar

2   spiced orange herbal tea bags

    Fresh or homemade whipped cream, for garnish

    Ground cinnamon, for garnish

In a medium saucepan, scald the milk and sugar by bringing it almost to a boil. Remove from heat and add the tea bags. Cover and steep, 5 minutes. Fish out the tea bags, pour the milk into mugs, and garnish with whipped cream and ground cinnamon. Yum!

Fresh Ginger-Infused Lemonade serves 6

I cannot imagine a long, hot summer without having a pitcher of this lemonade on standby at all times. I tend to lean toward the sweeter end of the lemonade spectrum. I don't care for that lip-puckering tartness that makes you look like a runway supermodel during fashion week. Feel free to experiment with this recipe until you find the perfect balance of sweet and tart that works for you.

1   cup sugar

1   (6-inch) piece of fresh ginger-root, peeled* and thinly sliced

Zest of 2 lemons, removed with a vegetable peeler

4¹/₂   cups water

2   cups freshly squeezed lemon juice (about 8 or 9 lemons)

Lemon slices, for garnish

In a medium saucepan, make a simple syrup by combining the sugar, ginger, lemon zest, and 1 cup of the water. Bring to a boil and immediately remove from heat. Set aside and let the mixture cool to room temperature. Strain out the solids. Pour the lemon juice into a pitcher; add the simple syrup and the remaining 3¹/₂ cups water. Give it a good stir, throw some lemon slices into the pitcher, and serve over ice.

*To peel ginger, use the edge of a spoon and move it along the curves of the root as if you're carving it. You'll be surprised at how easily the skin comes off, preserving the delicate flesh within.

Old-Fashioned New York Egg Cream serves 1

3 tablespoons good chocolate syrup (preferably Fox's U-Bet)

3 tablespoons heavy cream

8 ounces cold seltzer water

There are many theories on the correct way to make an authentic New York egg cream. I'm not from New York. I admit I have only been there a handful of times, and I am completely reliant on the childhood memories of a friend who grew up on Long Island. He told me there are three indelible truths when it comes to making the perfect egg cream. 1. If at all possible, you must use Fox's U-Bet chocolate syrup. I am told there simply is no substitute. (But just between you and me, I've used Hershey's and it's delicious.) 2. Heavy cream is better than milk. It adds an extra richness to the drink. 3. You must use ice-cold seltzer water. Apparently, club soda would be blasphemous.

In a tall glass, layer the chocolate syrup and the heavy cream. Pour the seltzer water over and stir vigorously.

Index

a

almond cookies, 166
appetizers, 22–56
    Asian beef lettuce wraps, 29
    black bean and corn salsa, 44
    brie, mango, and mint wraps with
        lime-cream dipping sauce, 32
    caramelized onion tartlets, 49
    chicken satay with spicy peanut dipping
        sauce, 43
    crispy calamari with orange-ginger dipping
        sauce, 40–41
    easy hummus, 45
    figs with goat cheese and port syrup, 51
    goat cheese torta strata, 24
    ham and Fontina mini-frittatas, 48
    iceberg wedges with real Thousand Island
        dressing, 35
    mini-cheeseburgers, 52
    mixed green salad with candied walnuts,
        Gorgonzola, and pears with champagne
        vinaigrette, 34
    oven-roasted salsa, 38
    pan-seared filet mignon with horseradish
        cream, 33
    pistachio-Parmesan truffles, 55
    prosciutto-wrapped asparagus, 39
    prosciutto-wrapped grilled plums with
        Gorgonzola and rosemary, 27
    real Maryland crab cakes with creamy herb
        remoulade, 42
    red-pepper jelly, 54
    stuffed mushrooms, 28
    sweet-and-sour cocktail meatballs, 25
    tomato-basil bruschetta, 56
    Vietnamese spring rolls with sweet and
        spicy dipping sauce, 30–31
    warm spinach salad with red grapes and
        pancetta, 36
    wild mushroom strudel, 46–47
apple cobbler, French, 169
apricot couscous, 122
artichokes, roasted, with sun-dried tomato aioli,
    128–29

arugula, pan-roasted New York strip steak with
    roasted red peppers, balsamic vinaigrette
    and, 104
Asian beef lettuce wraps, 29
Asian skirt steak, grilled, 93
asparagus:
    brown rice salad with mint and, 135
    penne with mushrooms and, 95
    prosciutto-wrapped, 39
avgolemono (chicken soup with lemon and egg
    sauce), 63
avocado soup, chilled, 61

b

bacon:
    and bean soup, easy, 151
    my favorite spinach salad with, 155
banana(s):
    cheesecake (chimpanzee), 173
    cream pie, old-fashioned, 182–83
    fritters with chocolate rum sauce, 160
    lemongrass, and coconut soup,
        Thai-inspired, 67
    molten chocolate cakes with raspberry
        puree and, 164–65
    nut bread, old-fashioned, 154
    -nut martini, 192
barley and wild mushroom soup, 66
basil:
    -cream sauce, chicken breasts with, 102
    -tomato bruschetta, 56
beans, canned:
    and bacon soup, easy, 151
    in pasta e fagioli, 64
    see also black beans
beef:
    chili-rubbed flank steak, 110
    grilled Asian skirt steak, 93
    John's coffee steak, 77
    lettuce wraps, Asian, 29
    in mini-cheeseburgers, 52
    pan-roasted New York strip steak with
        arugula, roasted red peppers, and
        balsamic vinaigrette, 104

pan-seared filet mignon with blackberry-Cabernet sauce, 100
pan-seared filet mignon with horseradish cream, 33
salt steak, 84
in shipwreck stew, 148
steak and red wine soup, 62
stew, cinnamon-kissed Moroccan, 108
in sweet-and-sour cocktail meatballs, 25
Thai marinated, 97
beverages, see cocktails
biscuits, old-fashioned herb and cheese, 133
black beans:
    and corn salsa, 44
    and mango salsa, 130
blackberry-Cabernet sauce, pan-seared filet mignon with, 100
black pepper, 14
blueberry scones, 181
breadcrumbs, 15
    lemony, broccoli with, 137
    panko, for oven-baked coconut shrimp with pineapple salsa, 103
breads:
    Aunt Judi's dinner rolls, 132
    blueberry scones, 181
    cinnamon chocolate scones, 181
    herbed Middle Eastern flat, 123
    old-fashioned banana nut, 154
    old-fashioned herb and cheese biscuits, 133
    old-fashioned zucchini, 156
brie, mango, and mint wraps with lime-cream dipping sauce, 32
broccoli with lemony breadcrumbs, 137
bruschetta, tomato basil, 56
Brussels sprouts, roasted, with crispy prosciutto, 124
butter, unsalted vs. salted, 16
butters, compound:
    cilantro-lime-chipotle, 139
    garlic, 139
    Gorgonzola, 138
    lemon-parsley, 138
    parsley-dill-lemon, 139
    tarragon, 138

C

cakes:
    chocolate decadence with raspberry puree, 176–77
    flourless chocolate, with orange-scented whipped cream, 170–71
    molten chocolate, with raspberry puree and bananas, 164–65
    old-fashioned carrot, 146
    sticky coconut, 167
    sticky orange juice, 149
    see also cheesecakes
calamari, crispy, with orange-ginger dipping sauce, 40–41
carrot cake, old-fashioned, 146
cheeseburgers, mini-, 52
cheesecakes:
    banana (chimpanzee), 173
    chocolate chip cookie dough, 168
    lemon white-chocolate, 161
chicken:
    breasts with basil-cream sauce, 102
    coconut soup, Thai, 69
    crepes, 88–89
    mango salad, 111
    my Mom's fried, 152
    orange-glazed, 115
    piccata, lemony, 114
    pot pie for grown-ups, 112–13
    satay with spicy peanut dipping sauce, 43
    tagine, Moroccan-inspired, 74
chickpeas, in easy hummus, 45
chili-rubbed flank steak, 110
chipotle-cilantro-lime butter, 139
chocolate:
    in black-bottom cupcakes, 180
    cake, flourless, with orange-scented whipped cream, 170–71
    cakes, molten, with raspberry puree and bananas, 164–65
    cinnamon scones, 181
    decadence with raspberry puree, 176–77
    martini, 190
    no-bake cookies, 142
    in old-fashioned New York egg cream, 199
    rum sauce, banana fritters with, 160
    soufflés, individual, 163

chocolate chip:
    cookie dough cheesecake, 168
    cookies, Neiman Marcus, 172
    oatmeal cookies, 145
cilantro-lime-chipotle compound butter, 139
cinnamon:
    chocolate scones, 181
    -kissed Moroccan beef stew, 108
clam(s):
    chowder, classic Manhattan, 70
    easy linguine with fresh herbs and, 81
cocktails, 186–99
    banana-nut martini, 193
    chocolate martini, 190
    Cosmopolitan, 191
    Creamsicle martini, 191
    Cuban mojito, 196
    the French martini, 190
    fresh ginger-infused lemonade, 198
    fresh watermelon martini, 193
    German chocolate cake martini, 195
    green apple martini, 189
    Key lime pie martini, 192
    limeade vodka, 196
    old-fashioned New York egg cream, 199
    pomegranate margaritas, 194
    pomegranate mojito, 197
    s'moretini, 193
    sparkling Shiraz from Down Under, 188
    spiced orange latte, 197
    tequila-fruit infusion, 195
    watermelon margaritas, 194
coconut:
    chicken soup, Thai, 69
    lemongrass, and banana soup,
        Thai-inspired, 67
    shrimp, oven-baked, with pineapple
        salsa, 103
    sticky, cake, 167
coffee steak, John's, 77
cookies:
    almond, 166
    chocolate no-bake, 142
    Neiman Marcus chocolate chip, 172
    oatmeal chocolate chip, 145
    peanut butter crisscross, 144
    snickerdoodles, 147
    Swedish, 143

cooking, carryover, 17
corn and bean salsa, 44
Cosmopolitan cocktail, 191
couscous, apricot, 122
crab cakes, real Maryland, with creamy herb
    remoulade, 42
cream, heavy:
    -basil sauce, chicken breasts with, 102
    in cream of macadamia nut soup, 65
    and white wine sauce, shrimp in, 94
    see also whipped cream
cream cheese frosting, for old-fashioned
    carrot cake, 146
crème brûlée, lavender, 179
crêpes, chicken, 88–89
Cuban mojito, 196
cupcakes, black-bottom, 180

d

desserts, 158–85
    Baked Alaska lemons, 175
    banana (chimpanzee) cheesecake, 173
    banana fritters with chocolate rum sauce, 160
    black-bottom cupcakes, 180
    blueberry scones, 181
    chocolate chip cookie dough cheesecake, 168
    chocolate decadence with raspberry purée,
        176–77
    flourless chocolate cake with orange-
        scented whipped cream, 170–71
    French apple cobbler, 169
    individual chocolate soufflés, 163
    lavender crème brûlée, 179
    lemon white-chocolate cheesecake, 161
    molten chocolate cakes with raspberry
        puree and bananas, 164–65
    old-fashioned banana cream pie, 182–83
    old-fashioned carrot cake, 146
    sticky coconut cake, 167
    sticky orange juice cake, 149
    strawberries in port, 178
    Watergate pie, 184–85
    see also cookies
dill-parsley-lemon butter, 139
dressings:
    balsamic vinaigrette, for pan-roasted New
        York strip steak with arugula and roasted

red peppers, 104

champagne vinaigrette, for mixed green salad with candied walnuts, Gorgonzola, and pears, 34

Thousand Island, iceberg wedges with, 35

for warm spinach salad with red grapes and pancetta, 36

dry ingredients, sifting of, 17

e

egg cream, old-fashioned New York, 199

eggs, 16

classic French omelette, 116–17

in a frame, 157

and lemon sauce, chicken soup with, 63

salad sandwiches, 150

see also frittatas

f

fennel, warm, and Parmesan salad, 127

figs with goat cheese and port syrup, 51

fish tacos, Baja-style fried, 106–7

Fontina and ham mini-frittatas, 48

French apple cobbler, 169

French mushroom soup, 71

frittatas:

ham and Fontina mini-, 48

zucchini-mushroom, 118

fritters, banana, with chocolate rum sauce, 160

g

garlic:

compound butter, 139

sautéed mushrooms with thyme and, 122

sautéed shrimp with butter, thyme, lemon and, 98

ginger:

-honey pork chops, 119

-infused lemonade, fresh, 198

-orange dipping sauce, crispy calamari with, 40–41

goat cheese:

figs with port syrup and, 51

torta strata, 24

Gorgonzola cheese:

compound butter, 138

prosciutto-wrapped plums with rosemary and, 27

gravy, for chicken crêpes, 88–89

Gruyère cheese sauce, sea scallops with, 105

h

ham and Fontina mini-frittatas, 48

ham hocks, in homemade split pea soup, 60

herb(s), herbed:

and cheese biscuits, old-fashioned, 133

-crusted pork tenderloin two ways, 78

-crusted rack of lamb with port demi-glace, 85

fresh, easy linguine with clams and, 81

fresh vs. dried, 14

marinated shrimp, 80

remoulade, creamy, for real Maryland crab cakes, 42

honey-ginger pork chops, 119

horseradish cream, pan-seared filet mignon with, 33

hummus, easy, 45

i

iceberg wedges with real Thousand Island dressing, 35

j

jelly, red-pepper, 54

k

kitchen equipment, 13–14, 17

kitchen tips, 14–21

kosher salt, 14

l

lamb, herb-crusted rack of, with port demi-glace, 85

latte, spiced orange, 197

lavender crème brûlée, 179

leeks with salmon in parchment paper, 92

lemon(y):

Baked Alaska, 175

breadcrumbs, broccoli with, 137

chicken piccata, 114
and egg sauce, chicken soup with, 63
-mint peas, 136
-parsley compound butter, 138
-parsley-dill compound butter, 139
sautéed shrimp with butter, garlic thyme
and, 98
white-chocolate cheesecake, 161
lemonade, fresh ginger-infused, 198
lemongrass banana, and coconut soup,
Thai-inspired, 67
lemon juice, fresh, 16
lime:
-cilantro-chipotle compound butter, 139
-cream dipping sauce, brie, mango, and
mint wraps with, 32
limeade vodka cocktail, 196
lime juice, fresh, 16
low-fat baking substitutes, 18

m

macadamia nut soup, cream of, 65
main dishes, 72–119
Baja-style fried fish tacos, 106–7
cheese ravioli with pumpkin sauce, 75
chicken breasts with basil-cream sauce, 102
chicken crepes, 88–89
chicken pot pie for grown-ups, 112–13
chili-rubbed flank steak, 110
cinnamon-kissed Moroccan beef stew, 108
cold-poached salmon with white nectarine
salsa, 96
easy linguine with clams and fresh herbs, 81
a few good eggs (classic French omelette),
116–17
fresh cheese ravioli with sage brown butter,
87
grilled Asian skirt steak, 93
herb-crusted pork tenderloin two ways, 78
herb-crusted rack of lamb with port demi-
glace, 85
herb-marinated shrimp, 80
honey-ginger pork chops, 119
John's coffee steak, 77
lemony chicken piccata, 114
mango chicken salad, 111
Moroccan-inspired chicken tagine, 74

mushroom ragu over soft polenta, 79
my Mom's fried chicken, 152
orange-glazed chicken, 115
oven-baked coconut shrimp with pineapple
salsa, 103
pan-roasted New York strip steak with
arugula, roasted red peppers, and
balsamic vinaigrette, 104
pan-seared filet mignon with blackberry-
Cabernet sauce, 100
penne with mushrooms and asparagus, 95
pistachio-crusted salmon filets, 83
salmon with leeks in parchment paper, 92
salt steak, 84
sautéed shrimp with butter, garlic, thyme,
and lemon, 98
seafood scampi, 86
sea scallops with Gruyère sauce, 105
shipwreck stew, 148
shrimp in white wine and cream sauce, 94
spaghetti alla carbonara, 90–91
sweet and spicy glazed salmon filets, 76
Thai marinated beef, 97
zucchini-mushroom frittata, 118
mango:
and black bean salsa, 130
brie, and mint wraps with lime-cream
dipping sauce, 32
chicken salad, 111
margaritas:
pomegranate, 194
watermelon, 194
marmalade, red-onion, 136
martinis:
banana-nut, 192
chocolate, 190
Creamsicle, 191
French, 190
fresh watermelon, 193
German chocolate cake, 195
green apple, 189
Key lime pie, 192
s'moretini, 193
meatballs, sweet-and-sour cocktail, 25
mint:
brie, and mango wraps with lime-cream
dipping sauce, 32

brown rice salad with asparagus and, 135
-lemon peas, 136
mojitos:
    Cuban, 196
    pomegranate, 197
Moroccan beef stew, cinnamon-kissed, 108
mushroom(s):
    penne with asparagus and, 95
    ragu over soft polenta, 79
    sautéed, with garlic and thyme, 122
    soup, French, 71
    stuffed, 29
    wild, and barley soup, 66
    wild, strudel, 46–47
    -zucchini frittata, 118

n

Neiman-Marcus chocolate chip cookies, 172

o

oatmeal chocolate chip cookies, 145
olive oils, 18
onion tartlets, caramelized, 49
orange:
    -ginger dipping sauce, crispy calamari with,
        40–41
    -glazed chicken, 115
    juice cake, sticky, 149
    -scented whipped cream, flourless chocolate
        cake with, 170–71

p

pancetta:
    in spaghetti alla carbonara, 90–91
    warm spinach salad with red grapes and, 36
Parmesan cheese:
    -pistachio truffles, 55
    and warm fennel salad, 127
parsley:
    -dill-lemon compound butter, 139
    -lemon compound butter, 138
pasta:
    Aunt Harriett's macaroni salad, 153
    cheese ravioli with pumpkin sauce, 75
    easy linguine with clams and fresh herbs, 81
    e fagioli (soup), 64
    fresh cheese ravioli with sage brown
        butter, 87
    penne with mushrooms and asparagus, 95
    spaghetti alla carbonara, 90–91
peanut butter crisscrosses, 144
peas, frozen green, 15
    lemon-mint, 136
pies:
    old-fashioned banana cream, 182–83
    Watergate, 184–85
pineapple:
    salsa, oven-baked coconut shrimp with, 103
    in tequila-fruit infusion, 195
pistachio:
    -crusted salmon filets, 83
    -Parmesan truffles, 55
plums, prosciutto-wrapped grilled, with
    Gorgonzola and rosemary, 27
polenta, soft, mushroom ragu over, 79
pomegranate:
    margaritas, 194
    mojito, 197
pork:
    chops, honey-ginger, 119
    tenderloin, herb-crusted, two ways, 78
    see also ham; pancetta; prosciutto
port wine:
    demi-glace, herb-crusted rack of lamb
        with, 85
    strawberries in, 178
    syrup, figs with goat cheese and, 51
potato(es):
    gratin, 125
    perfect mashed, 126
    twice-baked, 131
prosciutto:
    roasted Brussels sprouts with crispy, 124
    -wrapped asparagus, 39
    -wrapped grilled plums with Gorgonzola
        and rosemary, 27
pumpkin sauce, cheese ravioli with, 75

r

raspberry puree:
    chocolate decadence with, 176–77
    molten chocolate cakes with bananas and,
        164–65

red grapes, warm spinach salad with pancetta and, 36

red-onion marmalade, 136

red-pepper jelly, 54

red wine:
 Cabernet-blackberry sauce, pan-seared filet mignon with, 100
 sparkling Shiraz from Down Under, 188
 and steak soup, 62

rice, brown, salad with asparagus and mint, 135

rolls, Aunt Judi's dinner, 132

rosemary, prosciutto-wrapped grilled plums with Gorgonzola and, 27

rum chocolate sauce, banana fritters with, 160

S

sage brown butter, fresh cheese ravioli with, 87

salad(s):
 Aunt Harriett's macaroni, 153
 brown rice, with asparagus and mint, 135
 iceberg wedges with real Thousand Island dressing, 35
 mango chicken, 111
 mixed green, with candied walnuts, Gorgonzola, pears, and champagne vinaigrette, 34
 my favorite spinach, with bacon, 155
 warm fennel and Parmesan, 127
 warm spinach, with red grapes and pancetta, 36

salmon:
 cold-poached, with white nectarine salsa, 96
 filets, pistachio-crusted, 83
 filets, sweet and spicy glazed, 76
 with leeks in parchment paper, 92

salsas:
 black bean and corn, 44
 mango and black bean, 130
 oven-roasted, 38
 pico de gallo, for Baja-style fried fish tacos, 107
 pineapple, oven-baked coconut shrimp with, 103
 white nectarine, cold-poached salmon with, 96

salt steak, 84

sandwiches, egg salad, 150

sauces:
 basil-cream, chicken breasts with, 102
 blackberry-Cabernet, pan-seared filet mignon with, 100
 chipotle, for Baja-style fried fish tacos, 106–7
 chocolate rum, banana fritters with, 160
 creamy herb remoulade, real Maryland crab cakes with, 42
 Gruyère, sea scallops with, 105
 horseradish cream, pan-seared filet mignon with, 33
 lime-cream dipping, brie, mango, and mint wraps with, 32
 orange-ginger dipping, crispy calamari with, 40–41
 pumpkin, cheese ravioli with, 75
 sage brown butter, fresh cheese ravioli, 87
 spicy peanut dipping, chicken satay with, 43
 sun-dried tomato aioli, roasted artichokes with, 128–29
 sweet and spicy dipping, Vietnamese spring rolls with, 30–31
 white wine and cream, shrimp in, 94
 see also salsas

scallops
 sea, with Gruyère sauce, 105
 in seafood scampi, 86

scones, blueberry, 181

Shiraz, sparkling, from Down Under, 188

shrimp:
 herb-marinated, 80
 oven-baked coconut, with pineapple salsa, 103
 sautéed, with butter, garlic, thyme, and lemon, 98
 in seafood scampi, 86
 in white wine and cream sauce, 94

side dishes, 120–39
 apricot couscous, 122
 Aunt Judi's dinner rolls, 132
 broccoli with lemony breadcrumbs, 137
 brown rice salad with asparagus and mint, 135
 compound butters, 138–39
 herbed Middle Eastern flat bread, 123
 lemon-mint peas, 136
 mango and black bean salsa, 130
 old-fashioned herb and cheese biscuits, 133

perfect mashed potatoes, 126
potato gratin, 125
red-onion marmalade, 136
roasted artichokes with sun-dried tomato
    aioli, 128–29
roasted Brussels sprouts with crispy
    prosciutto, 124
sautéed mushrooms with garlic and
    thyme, 122
twice-baked potatoes, 131
warm fennel and Parmesan salad, 127
snickerdoodles, 147
sorbet, for baked Alaska lemons, 175
soufflés, individual chocolate, 163
soups, 58–71
    chicken, with lemon and egg sauce), 63
    chilled avocado, 61
    classic Manhattan clam chowder, 70
    cream of macadamia nut, 65
    easy bean and bacon soup, 151
    French mushroom, 71
    homemade split pea, 60
    pasta e fagioli, 64
    steak and red wine, 62
    Thai chicken coconut, 69
    Thai-inspired lemongrass, banana, and
        coconut, 67
    wild mushroom and barley, 66
sour cream-lime dipping sauce, for brie, mango,
    and mint wraps, 32
spinach:
    salad, warm, with red grapes and pancetta, 36
    salad with bacon, my favorite, 155
split pea soup, homemade, 60
spring rolls, Vietnamese, with sweet and spicy
    dipping sauce, 30–31
stocks, 15
strawberries in port, 178
strudel, wild mushroom, 46–47
Swedish cookies, 143
sweet-and-sour cocktail meatballs, 25

tacos, Baja-style fried fish, 106–7
tagine, Moroccan-inspired chicken, 74

tahini, in easy hummus, 45
tarragon butter, 138
tartlets, caramelized onion, 49
tequila-fruit infusion, 195
Thai chicken coconut soup (tom kha gai), 69
Thai marinated beef, 97
thyme:
    sautéed mushrooms with garlic and, 122
    sautéed shrimp with butter, garlic, lemon
        and, 98
tomato(es):
    -basil bruschetta, 56
    in classic Manhattan clam chowder, 70
    sun-dried, aioli, roasted artichokes with,
        128–29
tom kha gai (Thai chicken coconut soup), 69
torta strata, goat cheese, 24
truffles, pistachio-Parmesan, 55

Vietnamese spring rolls with sweet and spicy
    dipping sauce, 30–31

walnuts:
    crust, for Watergate pie, 184–85
    in old-fashioned banana nut bread, 154
watermelon:
    fresh, martini, 193
    margaritas, 194
whipped cream, 15
    orange-scented, flourless chocolate cake
        with, 170–71
white nectarine salsa, cold-poached salmon
    with, 96
white wine and cream sauce, shrimp in, 94
wraps:
    Asian beef lettuce, 29
    brie, mango, and mint, with lime-cream
        dipping sauce, 32

zucchini:
    -mushroom frittata, 118
    old-fashioned, bread, 156